The Uncovering Mythology Collection

A 2 in 1 Guide Into The World of Greek and Norse Gods and Goddesses, The Myths and The Legends

Lucas Russo

Uncovering Norse Mythology

A Beginner's Guide Into the World of Norse Mythology. Explore the Immortal Gods' Myths and History, Viking Warriors, and Magical Creatures

Lucas Russo

advice. The content within this book has been derived from various sources. Please consult a licensed professional before attempting any techniques outlined in this book.

By reading this document, the reader agrees that under no circumstances is the author responsible for any losses, direct or indirect, that are incurred as a result of the use of the information contained within this document, including, but not limited to, errors, omissions, or inaccuracies.

Table of Contents

Heil

I've come to the conclusion that mythology is really a form of archaeological psychology. Mythology gives you a sense of what a people believes, what they fear.

~ George Lucas

Oh, how we love to read mythology. At least, if Hollywood's adaptations of many of the Greek and Norse gods, heroes, and myths are any indication, we certainly do. We love to read about Thor, Freya, and Odin and all their amazing adventures. There is something in the ancient runic writing and oral tales that speaks to our deepest roots when we read or listen to Norse mythology.

In studying Norse mythology, I have found out about myths, the Norse gods and their personality traits, the apocalypse and creation stories, and fabulous creatures too. It is fascinating how an ancient culture has the power to influence popular culture today. From toys to movies, the ancient Norse gods and goddesses have risen once more. However, I find the Norse ways, stories, and myths truly inspiring (apart from being entertaining), don't you?

As renowned movie maker George Lucas said, mythology is an excavation of our psychology. What we read in myth and history tells us so much more about ourselves as humans than the mere wording in the ancient 13th century texts. It tells us about our own trials and tribulations too. We all want the courage of the handsome hammer wielding Thor or the wisdom of Odin, the one-eyed raven god. Even being in the presence of the massive runestones in Northern Europe or at the sites of the Viking ship graves in Norway has the power to move a deep part of our psyche.

From the Norse runic writing that dates back as far as 200-300 AD, making it some of the oldest runic writing sources on earth, we have managed to learn a great deal about the Norse culture and times. The Norse made sense of their world with the telling of great stories to inspire, delight, and educate their people. Just as we tuck our children into bed at night, I can just imagine a Norse dad also telling his child a bedtime story featuring the adventures of Thor or the deceptions of Loki.

Wanting to learn more about this fascinating culture and its accompanying traditions, I began extensive research, collecting stories, myths, and a vast glossary of uniquely beautiful old Norse words. As rugged and unforgiving as the Northern landscapes are, I found these stories to perfectly match an ancient people shaped by time, tragedy, and triumph.

How to Use This Book

This book is written not only to share Norse mythology with a curious mind. Instead, I have tried to create a comprehensive view of Norse mythology across the ages and how it survives even today. How you use this book is up to you as the reader. You can choose to skip to a chapter you are particularly interested in, such as the myths of the gods. However, I strongly recommend reading it cover to cover. You will find the experience so much more enriching. This is a complete overview of the gods, their characters, their inter-relatedness and how they affected the people their belief was founded on. Also, considering their effect on our modern society today will give you a much more nuanced view of the Norse gods, giants, creatures, themes, fates, and their stories.

So, if you're like me, you enjoy a sneak peek. You may already be familiar with some of the Norse myths or gods or stories, but here's what you can expect in the chapters that follow:

- **Once Upon a Time**

Find out who the Vikings were, what beliefs they held, and why their myths still survive till today. Discover the skalds or poets and explore the themes that we find in Norse myths, and consider how these themes can speak to our own lives today.

- **Norse Culture and Myth**

Find out more about the ways in which the oral traditions of the Vikings were recorded, their unique writing system, and how this affected their beliefs.

- **Where It All Began**

The best place to begin is in the beginning, and like Christianity and every other major religion on earth, Norse mythology has its own creation story, starting with a void. Here you can explore the Nine Realms, learn about the major gods, giants, creatures, and other forces that affected Norse mythology. Learn how the genealogy of the gods worked for and against them as alliances were crafted and enmities formed.

- **The Royal Family**

Norse mythology revolves around a few central figures, specifically the royal house of Asgard, and these gods deserve special mention. The characteristics and quirks of the gods are expanded on with tales specific to each god, where lessons are learned and history is made.

- **Asgardians**

The Asgardians included many powerful gods such as Tyr and Heimdall and influential gods like Idun. In an expansion on their abilities, skills, and challenges, you can get a real feel for these gods and how they will feature in the final days of Ragnarok.

- **The Vanir**

Having learned about the Aesir, it is important to also discover their arch enemies, the Vanir. By learning about Njord, Freya, and Freyr, you will learn how magic came to the Norse gods, and how making friends of your enemies can be rewarding in the end.

- **Deadly Offspring**

My love of myth often centered not only on the good guys, but it also thrived on the bad guys, and Norse myth has some of the best baddies around! We all love Loki's trickery from the Avengers movies, but I found the myths to be even better. I provide you with a detailed overview of Loki and his strange and dangerous children. It is in their own tragic and slightly demented tales that the seeds of fate are planted, leading up to the end of days and the twilight of the gods.

- **The End Times**

Final battles are always the most dramatic of events, and Ragnarok is the epitome of final conflicts. Discover the signs that hail the end of time, grip the edge of your tablet as you read about your hero's fate, and see the whole plot come together.

- **The Norse Gods Today**

When I wrote this book I was trying to find an ending, only to realize—it doesn't end. Norse mythology has no end. Not even in the sense of Ragnarok. Instead, it is resurrected and reborn with each generation in new and unusual ways.

- **Glossary**

And finally, I wanted to share the exciting and amazing words of Old Norse, what they mean, and some of the ways in which they were used in a glorious glossary that will gift you the skald tongue of Bragi. The glossary has a treasure trove of terms from Old Norse, along with their phonetic pronunciation (so you can sound like the Vikings did), with the emphasis bolded for easy use.

Why Read This Book?

In these digital pages, you will learn all about the major gods and goddesses of the ancient Nordic lore. I will share how the Nordic people believed the world was created and how they thought it might end. The Nordic people had a strange but advanced sense of how the world interacted, which they explained with their belief in the Nine Realms, connected by the World Tree called Yggdrasill. While the Nine Realms were each unique and separate, they all connected through this central trunk of the World Tree. I have always found this a beautiful metaphor for how we humans may be from different races and cultures, but that we all follow the same trunk from creation too.

The Norse myths were so strong and potent that they have been preserved even to today and still serve to entertain and educate many European cultures. The influences of these mythical stories still echo in the world today, and not just on the big screen or in comic books. Many of the same Viking greetings of old are still used today, and in 2018, a couple tied the knot in "the first Viking wedding in a thousand years" (Rach, 2018) with a ceremony presided over by a gothi (priest) and featuring longboats, hog roasting, blood offerings, and traditional throat singing.

From Norse myths, we learn about concepts like honor, valor, family, destiny, and time. We discover what sacrifice means, how tricksters can infiltrate our lives, and how we can master our time and our power to change our world. But the greatest power of these myths is the ability to make me want to read. I wanted above all to share that love with readers all over the world, who loved reading myths just like I do.

I grew up loving to read, but as life got busier, I read less and less, much to my great loss. Now, in my 30s, as a single guy interested in ancient histories and traditions like stoicism and the warrior's way, I have become passionate about self-development and mythology. Self-development and mythology may seem like a strange combination; it isn't. What you experience in yourself can be stimulated by myths and stories. Through myths we can discover new insights. This is, after all, where the hero's journey began. Renowned psychologist Joseph Campbell (1904, 11) so eloquently put it, "They're stories about the wisdom of life."

By reading Norse myths and the mythology of other ancient cultures, we learn things our modern world has not prepared us for. We lose a little part of what it means to be human in an age driven by technology, not magic; by equipment, not heroes. Reading mythology can help us dream again, reach into the very deepest parts of our psyche and discover our own inner hero again.

Reading these stories, I rediscovered the joy of storytelling and myth and the thrill of going on fantastical journeys with a childlike innocence. Like the Greek myths, these Norse myths have also shaped my concept of what it means to be a man in today's world. I would like to share those stories and influences with you here.

So, *Heil*—be healthy and happy—and *Til Árs ok Friðar*—a year of peace—as you travel along the World Tree with me.

Chapter 1:

Once Upon a Time

All good stories start with this phrase: once upon a time, or as in George Lucas' case, "a long time ago." The Viking era is, for practical purposes, documented as being from 793 AD lasting to 1066 AD, making it a relatively short-lived period in history. Yet, Vikings were documented through implication, if not specificity, in manuscripts earlier than 793 AD. We can also be fairly certain that their days extended beyond 1066 AD. It is simply that this period was their hey-day. The Norse traditions, which began with the Vikings, have expanded far beyond this time, persisting even today.

Reading the tales, myths, and traditions of the Vikings, the Norse gods they believed in, and thinking about how these influence us in our modern (but equally dangerous) world, makes for an enjoyable pastime.

Image 1: Image by WikiImages on Pixabay. Scandinavia, which includes Sweden, Norway, and Iceland, is the ancestral home of the Vikings.

Who Were the Vikings?

The Viking kings originated from Scandinavia, which is where they launched their fierce and much dreaded raids from. They raided up and down the British coastline, and also parts of Europe, even discovering North America more than 500 years before Christopher Columbus's trans-Atlantic voyage.

Vikings ruled the seas. They were the first major sea-faring nation, and definitely one of the first to use their longboats to attack and raid other nations. Their longboats were so important to their culture that they would bury a Viking's boat with him. Today, Norway has several historically preserved longboats in their museums. And in 2018, a Viking ship graveyard was discovered where whole ships had been buried on land during the Viking era.

But back to ancient Viking times. The Vikings were so influential to European history that I was astounded to learn their conquest of nations meant not ruin, but civilization. Peoples conquered by the Vikings developed laws and learned to write in runic script, and the Vikings brought concepts about trade and commerce that had previously not existed. The Viking conquest of Eastern Europe led to the Rus empire, which became known as Russia today (McCoy, n.d.-a).

As you might imagine, a people so advanced and well-traveled as the Vikings would have a rich history, filled with stories and beliefs that lasted well past their own empire. Much of this history and storytelling happened in an oral tradition, but fortunately, the Vikings were also given to recording their histories, events, and stories on runestones, and many of these were later recorded into Latin once the Vikings' descendants were conquered by the Roman empire. Thanks to these scripts, we have a strong recorded history for the Viking or Norse kingdoms and their traditions.

While the Vikings were known as seafarers, they were also farmers, and most of their homesteads in Scandinavia were constructed to farm, produce food, and give shelter in times of famine and disease. When the prime days of Viking raids ended with the creation of sea forts to protect the British Isles, the Vikings turned to trade routes. Many of the Viking warriors went from raiders to caravan guards, traveling as far east and south as Baghdad.

With travel and trade, the Vikings were known to keep slaves or serfs (servants) as property. Their society consisted of three tiers:

Nobles

Firstly, the noble lords (earls) owned large sections of land that were worked by their subjects. These lords were responsible for caring for their subjects, keeping them safe, ruling in the cases of disputes, and enforcing the law. They, in turn, paid taxes to the kings who ruled the lands. The earls or chieftains gained power through military victories such as raids and dominating their neighbors.

Free Men

The second tier of Viking society was the free men. These were smaller landowners who lived independently, fending for themselves, and being responsible for their own well-being.

Slaves/Serfs

The last tier comprised slaves or serfs who had to work submissively for the landowners who owned them or owned their service. The members of this tier had little power or entitlement, but they were still reasonably well-treated, and they were given a place at the hearth to stay and enjoy safety and protection.

What Is Norse Mythology?

Norse mythology is a collection of the stories, beliefs, customs, and the history of the Germanic-speaking peoples of Northern Europe. Essentially, it is an amalgamation of the myths and stories of the pre-Christian Germanic people and their cultures from Denmark, Finland, Iceland, Sweden, and Norway. Once Christianity took hold, the Norse beliefs began to wane.

However, today, we can still see influences of Norse mythology in our world. Even the days of the week stem from Norse mythology with Tuesday being Tyr's day, Thursday being Thor's day, and Friday being known as Freya's day.

How Did the Myths Survive?

What we know about the Norse or Viking mythology is mostly extrapolated from two ancient texts compiled in the Middle Ages in Iceland. These texts are known as *the Poetic Edda* or *Elder Edda.* They contained Norse history and myth captured in poetic form. While nobody knows exactly who the author or creator of these manuscripts were, it is known that they captured the history and beliefs of the Norse culture from 800 AD to 1270 AD. The claim is that the chieftain Snorri Sturluson wrote these collections of poems and battle songs around 1222 AD.

The most famous of these poems is "Völuspá" (meaning Sibyl's prophecy), which was a lengthy poem covering the shaping of the world and the prophesied ending or Armageddon that would come with Ragnarok or the final battle.

Much of Norse mythology is contained in the "Völuspá." It is where we learn about the polytheistic religious views of the Norse. The ancient Vikings and Norse cultures believed in as many as 66 deities. Some of these were mightily renowned, from Odin to Freya and Heimdall to Thor and Loki. But some deities were lesser known and only featured occasionally in the great saga of Norse mythology.

There are also other less well-known texts that contain Icelandic poetry, which refer to mythic events or figures such as Odin or the Valkyrie. Even family histories were interspersed with mythological subjects. What we see as fiction today was considered fact and religion to the ancient Norsemen. Heroes and legends were recorded as faithfully as births and deaths. For the ancient Norsemen, it was as if Odin himself (and many other gods and goddesses) walked among them daily.

The first actual historical account that was recorded was begun in the 1200s and was compiled by a Danish scholar known as Saxo Grammaticus. In this account, he recorded the history of the Danish people as well as their pagan gods and the ancient heroes they believed in. In turn, Grammaticus was recorded along with some mention of his work in the Roman and medieval historians' works. And so, history began to record the world of the Vikings and their rich tapestry of myths, gods, tales, songs, battles, and otherworldly kingdoms, all arranged along the World Tree.

The Skalds—Poets and Bards

History was recorded in poetic form. Prose writing style didn't feature as strongly as later Latin history records were wont to do. This might have been since singing was a powerful part of Scandinavian and Norse culture. Since it is easier and more entertaining to sing poems around the hearth, the role of the bard or *skalds* took on new prominence in Norse society. The skalds were permanently at the different courts and long halls of the lords, earls, chieftains, and kings of the Norse lands. Most of these were Icelandic by the 11th century, which is why so much of Norse recorded history and myth is Icelandic in origin today.

Since these myths were orally presented through singing and performances, there was quite a lot of variation in the recounting of the tales and legends. Each skald was likely to create their own flavor of myth dependent on what their lord liked to hear. However, with the discovery of the *Poetic Edda* in the later 11th century, there emerged a more standard version of the myths and histories of the earlier Norse accounts.

Writing started to dominate, and many myths were recorded into Latin by skalds. History and myth began to spread more widely, influencing more cultures and peoples throughout Europe. Who could resist the poetic presentations of the adventures of Thor or the mighty justice of Odin or the beauty of the fickle Freya? This was more than the entertainment of the day—it was their education system too.

Major Themes and Myths

Through songs and recitations, the Norse people learned their history, culture, and myths. The stories usually had definite themes that were used to teach values to the people. Common themes emerged based on the living experience of the Norse people:

Bravery Despite Harshness

This is an overarching theme in Norse mythology. No matter the odds you faced, you were expected to be brave and steadfast in an emulation of the warrior code. While this may seem depressing, it was aimed at motivating the people by telling them that everyone has a harsh fate, even the gods. In the barren northern wastelands with its cold and unforgiving landscape where hunger and conflict was often a daily existential experience, the consolation that even the gods suffered helped people face up to their challenges. This theme encompassed the acceptance of your fate with courage and bravery. Honor was to be found at the end of a harsh journey or trying existence. Complaining about life wasn't something the Norse did.

Everything Ends

Norse mythology has different and powerful gods and goddesses, but they are also very human and they also die. While they are sometimes reborn, they are not truly immortal and also have to face the end of the world. This concept helped prepare the common man, woman, and child for the reality of death. In the harsh environment of the northern lands, death was a daily reality, and only by living bravely could you be assured of being remembered.

Even Gods Don't Always Win

Greek and Roman mythology created a picture of immovable and completely aloof gods who were drunk on their own power, believing they would live forever. In stark contrast, the Norse gods and goddesses were almost human in their characteristics. They knew they didn't have everything under their ultimate control and they accepted that things would go wrong. Sons betrayed fathers, and brothers slew brothers, and other real-life themes were often experienced by the Norse gods. This made the Norse people experience their gods as more than human but still relatable. Like humans, the Norse gods knew they would one day die.

Creation

Image 2: Image by Yuriy Chemerys on Unsplash. When considering the rugged and unforgiving landscapes of the Scandinavian countries, it becomes quite a haunting experience to listen to their creation myths read or sung aloud.

The creation myth was a powerful story that helped Norse people come to terms with their lives, accept their environment, and continue striving to reach their potential. The story begins with a place that was empty and deep; it had existed before anything else did. This endless abyss was known as Ginnungagap where there was endless silence and darkness. Lying between the homeland of elemental fire and the homeland of elemental ice (between Niflheim and Muspelheim), this endless abyss is where the cosmos was spawned and where it will one day collapse and end.

In the creation myth, frost and flames met in Ginnungagap, where the fire melted the ice. The resulting drops became the frost giant Ymir, and the thawing ice became a cow, nourishing him. This cow licked salt blocks, freeing the first man, Buri.

Buri had married Bestla, the daughter of a frost giant, and they had three sons, Odin, Vili, and Vé. According to mythic legend, the three sons killed the frost giant Ymir, making the world from his corpse.

The frosty and mountainous landscape of Scandinavia indeed makes one think of the body of a frosty giant slain in some terrible battle, and it is then no surprise that such a strange story would be their creation myth.

Image 3: Image by ella peebles on Unsplash. The end of days myth is like most such myths apocalyptic in nature, and the world ends in a mighty battle between fire and ice.

End of the World … Ragnarok

The end of the world in Norse mythology is a series of terrible events as foretold by the poem "Völuspá." In the poem, the frost and fire giants unite against the gods and man in a final battle that destroys everything, sinking the world under a great sea. After many years, the earth will resurface, and the surviving gods will join together. The world will be repopulated by the last two human survivors.

This is a typical doomsday prediction, with the world ending in fire and ice. Yet, it is fascinating that it is humans who will repopulate the earth, not the gods who will magically save it. Instead, the message is to embrace your fate, even if that fate is to die. Even the gods die.

~~~~~//~~~~~

The Norse beliefs may not have purely religious value today, but aside from their entertainment factor, they offer unique insights into our own humanity. They allow us to consider our own belief in creation, end of days prophecies, and concepts such as personal honor, valor, and bravery. It's time to see where it all began ...

Chapter 2:

Norse Culture and Myth

The Norse culture and myth is still very much alive and present in the Scandinavian countries of the world. While you can go on tours of the sacred sites in Norway, Sweden, and even Denmark, you can also learn about these cultural traditions today through an amazing network of sites online and through social media. But let's look a little further back at how the information we do have about the Norse gods and their lives have come to us.

Recording Norse Histories

Much of the early Norse histories, beliefs, traditions, and cultural expressions have not been recorded accurately. Resources from that time are somewhat limited. The ancient Norse were given to an oral tradition. This meant they remembered their history instead of recording it. Only later as the Vikings progressed to creating a complex system of runes to record their history did the concept of "writing" enter Nordic culture.

These runes were mostly created and read by the Norse priests, shamans, and bards or skalds. The common folk didn't know how to read runes, which imbued the runes with a mystical power. They were said to be signs of power, and these runes were often carved into wood, stone, and bone as charms of protection that were worn by warriors and common folk alike. Today still, the use of runic pendants as jewelry is popular among those who favor the ancient traditions. Runes also feature prominently in full body tattoos that are quite popular among the more traditional Norse descendants.

The *Poetic Edda* and the *Prose Edda* are two volumes created by the Icelandic scribe Snorri Sturluson, who recorded the poems and stories from the Viking era during the 13th century. While he faithfully recorded what he read and translated from the runestones found all across Northern Europe, Snorri was of Christian origins, making some of his records somewhat biased against traditional Norse concepts and beliefs.

One primary source for information that Snorri used was from the medieval manuscript known as the Codex Regius. The *Poetic Edda* contained a number of poems that were copied from the rune stones and the Codex Regius, including "Völuspá," "Lokasenna" and "Hlöðskviða."

Reading the Runes

The ancient runes, not to be confused with the ancient ruins, offer both knowledge and visual appeal and presence. Visiting any of the standing stone sites and seeing the runes first-hand can have a profound effect on you.

Runes are symbols that represent a type of alphabet that are arranged to create words or concepts. To make matters a little more complicated, there were also many different runic alphabets, which meant different interpretations when these were later translated into the Latin alphabet.

The power of runes is that they make visible the sound of simple units called phonemes. Each rune, like the alphabet, is a visual representation of a sound. This concept was like magic to the early Norse, who had never seen people produce sounds from symbols before. The conceptualization of rune creation as magic is also represented in myth through the act of making fate depicted as weaving or rune carving.

While each rune represented a sound such as "A," they each also had a name that represented something else. So, the rune for the sound "F" was called Fehu, which meant "cattle." The rune for the sound or phoneme "Th" was called Thurisaz, which meant "giant." Apart from meaning "giant," it also implied "suffering and danger."

Reading the runes was, therefore, more of an art than a science as the runic meanings are constructed from sight and sound. There is certainly a magical quality to the runes, and no magical tale is complete without runes or some other magical inscription.

The presence of runes is found in many of the Norse myths. Odin learns to read the runes carved on the trunk of Yggdrasil, while Bragi, the famed skald is said to have runes etched on his tongue, which might be where the expression "to have a silver tongue" comes from.

Runes provide an intriguing glance back into the past, but it is a time that is made up of history and magical that we see.

Norse Beliefs

The Norse had a wide range of beliefs, and many of these still have some relevance today. However, I wanted to look specifically at the cornerstone beliefs of ancient Norse culture. Here are a few pivotal views that these antique warriors and their families held to:

- **Fate**

For the Norse, fate (old Norse word: Urðr) set the path before your feet to walk in life. While you may try to step off that path, or hide in a hole, you would still end up at the same end. The belief was that all living things, including the gods, were tied to their fates. Whether you accepted it or fought against it, your fate was your fate.

The only beings who were outside of fate were the Norns, who created fate. Practitioners of the Norse magic known as seidr could sometimes get glimpses into the future, seeing what fate had in store. What is markedly different between Norse and Christian views on fate was that the Norse saw fate as being completely a-moral and there was no good or evil, right or wrong. There was simply your place in time.

Talking to the Norns or trying to influence your fate was quite like talking to a tree as they had no interest in any attempts to sway fate. Since fate was so out of the hands of the humans, gods, or giants, it lends a certain tragic feeling to the Norse myths.

While the Viking view on fate may seem defeatist, it is far from that. Your fate is not something you simply passively accept. Instead, it is about riding into battle with courage, even if the outcome is known. In modern day life, this could be seen as accepting the potentially bad hand of cards you are dealt and still striving to achieve greatness before the end.

- **Magic of the Seidr**

Viking or Norse magic was known as seidr. It was a form of shamanism that, while it accepted fate, believed it could make some minor changes. So, if a warrior's fate was to die in battle, then a seidr shaman could help that warrior to first vanquish their enemy and then die in battle. The aim of a seidr practitioner was usually to bring about prophecy, send a blessing, or invoke a curse. The Norns used seidr magic to create fate, so the two forces were intertwined. Both Odin and Freya were accomplished practitioners of the seidr. Traditionally, seidr magic was a woman's activity, and all three Norns were female. Yet, Odin was proficient at it too, and it's suggested in some ancient texts that Odin was temporarily kicked out of Asgard for practicing a woman's art, namely magic. The act of weaving, which is involved in practicing seidr magic, is a woman's art. Weaving makes this form of magic practice extremely ill-suited to men.

In Norse culture, the term "völva" is used to define a woman who is a practitioner of seidr magic, and this woman is both revered and shunned. The völva lived outside of society, yet she also participated in it.

Norse beliefs held that all living things had spirit, which extended to plants and animals too. Hence, these could be influenced by magic. This gave the practitioners of magic the ability to control things like animals, plants, and even the weather. Due to the magical nature of the forces at work in Norse times, dreams were taken very seriously. So, when Baldur had a nightmare about his own death, it was taken very seriously by his mother, Frigg, who was herself a seidr practitioner.

- **Their Sense of Self**

In modern day psychology, we have learned the theory that our sense of self is made up of three parts: the ego, the id, and the superego. Most commonly, we see ourselves as having a body, a mind, and a spirit. The Vikings had a slightly different view on their sense of self, which supports their shamanistic practices and cosmological beliefs.

For the ancient Norse, the self was made of many different parts, and some of these could work on their own, or they could even detach from the rest and leave the body for a while before returning. While there is no definitive answer as to just how many and what kind of parts constitute the self in Norse beliefs, these are some of the more commonly acknowledged ideas:

The Hamr

(meaning: skin)

It is something you look like, your appearance. Since hamr can change, this is the core word or concept at Norse shapeshifting. When changing your appearance, the term skipta hömum (meaning: changing hamr) is used.

The Hugr

(meaning: thought or thinking)

The Norse believed your thinking can help you connect to other people without your conscious thought leaving your body. This might be related to some form of astral projection or speaking to someone over great distances with the power of your mind.

The Fylgja

(meaning: an attendant spirit)

When the Norse had animals who helped them, they could use these animals as a kind of second sight or familiar gift. Ravens, cats, and all manner of animals could be seen as being someone's fylgja. Odin had two ravens, Hugin and Munin, that he could interact with and gain information about the outside world. These animals or attending spirits are seen as part of the person's self.

The Hamingja

(meaning: luck or talent)

The Norse believed the luck or talent of an ancestor could be separated from their self upon death, and it was this part that was reincarnated in a relative. Even without death, a person's hamingja could be temporarily lent to someone. That person would gain the talent and insight of the person whose haminja they have acquired temporarily.

This concept tied into their beliefs, and warriors might implore a god such as Thor to lend them his hamingja for a battle. When imbued with Thor's power, the warrior was said to have the god's strength and skill. Those who claimed Thor as their family god might have more of a sense of warrior-spirit in them than the Norse who claimed a softer god or goddess like Frigg.

● Their Belief in the Afterlife

The Norse didn't really have a well-defined sense of the afterlife. Some sources claim that the spirit goes on to a spirit hall such as Valhalla or even Hel's hall upon death. In the world of the dead, the spirits did the same things they did in real life too. They dueled, drank and ate, and they practiced their magic more. It's not quite clear how a soul was picked to go to Valhalla or Helheim, but the choosing seemed to have something to do with whether the dead were warriors or lived plain lives.

The warriors went to Valhalla if they died honorably in battle. Those who died without a sword in their hands were probably sent to Helheim. This might also be why Viking warriors were burned with their sword in their hands when they died. However, historians quickly point out that we only have this distinction between Valhalla and Helheim due to the early Christian scholar Snorri Sturluson who recorded most of the Viking myths and runes in the *Poetic Edda*.

There was also a belief among early Vikings that the dead can be reborn into a relative. Thus, when Thor died, he could have been reborn into one of his sons. This is quite likely as there are some accounts of Viking myth that indicates the fallen gods would be reborn again.

Lastly, there is also no concept of punishment or reward for life in death with the Vikings. They didn't believe you went to Helheim as punishment or to Valhalla as reward. Instead, it was simply another place to exist in. The idea of heaven and hell were very Christian and didn't feature in Viking myth until much later in the Norse history when Christianity had begun pollinating Nose culture with biblical beliefs.

- **Why Choose These Gods**

As I stood on the blackened volcanic soils of Iceland, I looked at the great burial mounds and the museums that abound throughout the countryside, and I found myself wondering what had made the Norsemen of antiquity come up with the gods they did. Why Odin, Thor, Freya, and Baldur? Why does any culture come up with the gods that are so particular to their beliefs?

While Christianity believes that God made man in His image, the Norse mythological system might be the other way around. The Norse peoples had to find a way to explain their amazing countryside, make sense of warring tribes, and bring some sense of belonging and order to their physical existences. So, by creating and believing in gods like Odin, Thor, and Heimdall, the Vikings were making gods that they could turn to in times of need, gods who would represent the land, and gods who inspired acceptance of a harsh lifestyle. After all, if the gods could accept their own fate to die in battle, then surely the humans could accept their own fate to survive or perish in harsh winters, to win or lose in battle, and show courage in the face of adversity.

Traditional Viking Daily Living

How would the gods have impacted the lives of the ancient Vikings? Let's look a little closer at a traditional Viking's days with the gods:

Sven is a typical Viking. He lives on a small landholding with his family, and their household god is Freyr, since they are blessed with many children and live closer to the land. Life is tough, and in summer, they eke out a living from a rocky patch of land that is fertile but hard to farm due to the limitations of the agricultural tools of the time. His oldest son, Erik, who is 10 years old, fishes in the local fjord for trout, eel, and other fish to add to their diet as they can't slaughter the livestock regularly. While Sven had seven cows, which was quite a nice herd for a lowly farmer, he had lost five to the raiders from nearby villages. They had also sold two of his children into slavery when they raided and stole the children.

Their small home is a roundhouse made of turf since they can't afford timber, and trees are scarce in this part of Norway. There's a central fire pit, and the fire is kept going throughout the day and night to warm up their home. This is also where their cooking takes place. At night, they sleep in a circle around the fire, their feet pointing towards the coals.

It is not an easy lifestyle, but Sven doesn't grumble. Even the gods face their challenges, and he will face his too. He knows his fate is to die in battle, for aside from farming in summer, he also participates in Viking raids in late summer before returning home before the deepest snows of winter. He joins a local warband, and they raid the shores of the nearby British Isles. The objective is to gather gold, precious gems, textiles, and other valuables that can add to his wealth and be sold to buy essentials for his family.

Going on raids presents opportunities to gain wealth, esteem, and honor as he can distinguish himself on the battlefield and please the gods. After the battles, they honor the dead, taking them home for burial near the small town. Sven is happy with the warband he is in as their leader is a good man who follows the ways of Odin.

He is wise, first scouting out an area they want to raid, and he will always look for ways to win that will not cost his men their lives. They aren't afraid to die. What warrior wouldn't want to be blessed by the Valkyrie and taken to Odin's hall in Valhalla? But they all have families, and if they fall in battle, who will protect their families from other raiders?

The eve before battle, Sven prays to his gods. He asks Thor for courage and power. Odin, he asks for wisdom and strategy. Freya, he asks for protection as she can use the seidr magic to cast a spell of protection over him. Sven also asks for luck and blessings from his ancestors, whom he honors daily.

Battle upon battle, the warband fights, wins, and gains glory. Sven is soon quite rich for a farmer, and he can purchase another three cows to enlarge his herd. This also means more work though, and he hires two young men to help him in running his farm. He also buys a slave at the market to help plough up the more difficult fields for planting.

To ensure a good crop, Sven pays a local priest of Freyr to come and bless his land. While they are ploughing the land, the priest walks over the newly turned soil, sprinkling apple cider or mead over the ground. He also asks for the last ear of corn from the previous harvest, which he threshes with a sharp knife and scatters to the four corners of the wind. The priest now announces that the land is blessed by Freyr himself and a good crop will grow. This ritual also shows the delicate relationship the Norsemen had with the land spirits.

At night, Sven tells his children the stories of the gods, always including a little lesson for them. He tells them of Odin's sacrifice by hanging on the Tree of Life, and here he teaches them to always be resolute in their wishes. Odin hung for nine days; how many humans could have said or done the same? These tales are meant to teach and inspire the children.

When it's bedtime, Sven and his wife, Hilga, tuck the children in. While they fold in the woven blankets, they mutter a traditional blessing over the head of each child. The boys, Sven mentions to his house god, Freyr. But the girls, he mentions to Freya.

At the start of the next winter, Sven is blessed with another child, but he is still off raiding. During the birth, the local women gather and sing songs to Frigg and Freya, asking for healing and health for the child and mother. Sven is not yet back from the raids, and the family prays for his safe return. They pray to Njord for fair weather as they wait for Sven and the other warriors to return. Finally, nine days after the birth, Sven marches over the nearby hill. Luckily, he was just in time as he only had nine days to get home, for on the ninth day, he had to hold his child on his knee and name the babe.

Sven names his new boy, Thorian. Choosing a name that is based on the god of lightning is due to an omen that Sven experienced. He had been walking home when he saw a lightning streak flash over the sky above a rune stone. When he returned from a fierce battle to learn his child had been born, he saw it as a gift from Thor. While away raiding, Sven had been sorely pressed during a battle, and he had prayed to Thor to help him defend his comrades and win victory. Victory had been granted, and Sven now believed that Freyr may have been off on an adventure and didn't hear his pleas, so Thor had answered instead.

Winter is long, and back at home, there is little to do outside as most of the land is covered thickly by snow and ice. The livestock sleep inside with the family who will care for them in separate little camps inside the home. The family survives off the grain they harvested in summer, the fish they caught and salted, and what meat they could cure and store. While waiting for the winter months to blow over, the family talks about their ancestors, recount tales of the gods, and they may even have performed mini plays about the gods. This is also a time for the women to weave cloth and repair clothing. The men might mend nets, carve runes on stone and wood, and if they were skillful enough, they might make weapons or tools with some minor metal work. These weapons would probably be consecrated by using a blessing or calling on the approval of the family god.

During the following summer, Sven makes offerings of mead and fresh meat to the land spirits or wights, ensuring they are content with the new field he is ploughing. If he does not do this, he may anger them, causing crops to fail or disease to strike.

Near the end of that summer, his son, Thorian, falls seriously ill. They call on a traveling völva to come and help them. This requires deep magic and beyond their normal rituals that the family performs. At the völva's instruction, Sven buys a boar from the market, which he slaughters in a ritual sacrifice in the meadow beyond his house to appease a restless spirit that has poisoned his son. The völva works ancient land magic known as seidr, and she calls on the healing powers of the land. Reading the child's fate, she knows the boy is not meant to die before he reaches manhood.

She tells Sven and his family to pray to Eir, who is considered a goddess of healing (though she was thought to have been Frigg's handmaiden). His prayer might have been something like this:

Hail Eir, goddess of healing who sits on the hill. *Heil*, healer, physician, and keeper of ill children. We implore you, Eir, shelter this needy child. Heal this sick child. Bring a remedy with your soft voice, and shower blessings with your gentle eyes. May you bring health and vitality to this child. Make him hale and whole again. Eir, we call to you, we call to you.

The boy may or may not recover; either way, the gods are thanked for his life (or death) and honored. To the Vikings, death was not a bad thing, though they would then mourn that the boy died of illness and not in battle with a sword in his hand.

Sven thanks the gods and goddesses daily for looking after his farm, and much of what he does is to build a reputation and ensure his stature as a warrior, which will earn him a seat in the halls of Valhalla.

The Telling of Tales

Before we get into the tales and characters of Norse mythology, I wondered why and how these stories might have been told, and Neil Gaiman's interview with Shadow Writer might hold the answer to these questions. Brown (2012) relates how Gaiman believes the writer of the *Poetic Edda* Snorri Sturluson might have sat around a fire with his friends sharing a tale such as "The Meeting of the Utgard-Loki Giant."

Thor, Loki, and Thor's servant (a human boy named Thjalfi) were traveling to Jotunheim. They were always looking for adventure and trouble in equal measure. Reaching a deep forest, the three were ready to make camp for the night but saw a set of caves instead. The caves were interlinked with a large central chamber and smaller side chambers, almost like a house. They decided to spend the night there.

During the night, there was suddenly a massive earthquake, and the very walls of the cave seemed to buckle and shake. Terrified, the gods and the human boy held onto their belongings and each other as they waited for the inevitable end. But morning came, and they walked out of the caves unscathed.

(Snorri might have spoken dramatically or shaken the dining room table if the story was being told at dinner.)

The next morning, as the companions stepped into the bright sunlight, they saw a giant that was far bigger than anything they had ever seen before. Even the mighty Thor was cowed, and he politely asked after the giant's name.

"Oh, but I know who you are! You are the mighty Thor … although you are a lot smaller than I imagined!" the giant said, laughing as he reached behind them and picked up the caves. "What were you doing in my glove?"

(Snorri might roar with laughter here, and there would be chuckles all around the beer hall of the Icelandic castle in the 13th century as he told this part.)

Thor and the giant soon struck up a conversation, and Thor explained that he, Loki, and the serving boy were looking for adventures in the realm of Jotunheim. They wanted some trolls to kill or … uhm, large creatures to slay.

(Snorri would be sure to look embarrassed as he pretended to be Thor telling the giant how they were looking for giants to kill.)

Well, the unnamed giant seemed kindly enough. Most giants would simply jump in and try to slay the heroes, but this giant decided to travel to a nearby castle where there were adventures to find.

At the castle, a giant king welcomed them, telling them how they could stay if they could each best a giant at something using their best talents. Thor instantly claimed to be the biggest drinker, while Loki said he could eat faster than anyone, and the servant said he could run like the wind. Their giant opponents approached, and Thor drank from the mead horn of the giant king, hardly able to drain the mead away from the brim. Meanwhile, the king drained his horn with one gulp. Loki began eating at the end of one trestle table with an assortment of meats laid out. Another giant began in the middle. They would see who could eat fastest.

After a few minutes, Loki was completely full, but looking up, he was surprised and awed to see the giant had eaten more than three quarters of the meat, bones, sinew, and even the table, clearly winning.

Thjalfi was next to race against a giant, who within the first few strides far out distanced the human boy, leaving him winded and in the dust. Thus, the three companions lost, and they felt quite miserable. After all, the gods weren't used to losing!

(Snorri might pause here to allow the mostly Christian audience to have a laugh at the expense of the pagan gods.)

The giant king of the castle suddenly turned into the unnamed giant from the forest, and he explained the following:

Loki's opponent had actually been fire, which could consume everything faster than any man could. The boy Thjalfi had run his race against thought, and there was nothing faster than thought. Thor had been competing against eternity. While you could conquer small amounts of it, you would never beat eternity.

In telling tales such as this one, there may have been a moral implication or some form of entertainment to be had. The Norse gods weren't all serious and high minded. Likewise, the early Vikings had a broad sense of humor too, and they were likely to tell mythological tales as entertainment and learning material.

I am reminded again, as a child of the eighties, that the Vikings didn't have modern day entertainment like the internet or TVs. They would gather around fires, listening to the bards or skalds weave stories that transported their minds to Asgard and Jotunheim where they were momentarily relieved of their often harsh realities. This is why the myths of the Norse gods have persisted to today. They meet some human need to challenge ourselves, learn from dramas and challenges, and become more, earning our place in Asgard too.

~~~~~//~~~~~

What is also unique about the bond between the Vikings and their gods is that they could serve different gods at the same time, and they could also willfully disobey their gods. There was no punishment for disobeying a god, and unlike the Greek gods, there was hardly ever any punishment for not obeying your god(s). The Vikings saw their gods as divine beings but also human beings whom they could empathize with, relate to, and learn from.

Chapter 3:

Where It All Began

All cultures and religions have their own creation stories, detailing the way in which they believe it all began. Their version of the beginning is often a powerful indication of how that culture's members see their role in the order of things. The Norse are no different. Let's take a look at how the Norse believed the world to have begun, what creatures they saw as being created at that time, and how their belief in the nine worlds tied everything together.

Image 4: Image by Jeremy Bishop on Unsplash. The Viking or Norse belief in a world tree that connects the nine worlds is at the center of their religious beliefs about creation.

The Creation Myth

According to Norse mythology, in the beginning there was also a great void. Much like the Christian Genesis story, Norsemen believed there was nothing except the void that existed between the elemental fires of Muspelheim and the elemental frost of Niflheim. One might think of these as the first two worlds on the World Tree. Like fruit, connected to a tree, these realms existed independently but were joined by the World Tree.

In the vast emptiness of Ginnungagap (meaning: the great emptiness), the fires of Muspelheim and the frost of Niflheim met, and in this meeting, there was an exchange. Fire melted ice, and from these drops of the first waters, Ymir or the first of the frost giants was formed. These giants would form a godlike race known as the Jötnar.

Image 5: Image by LoggaWiggler from Pixabay. The giants or Jötnar had terrible powers, and their elemental natures hinted at a time of chaos.

Fortunately, the frost giant Ymir slept, as giants usually do in these creation stories. But while he slept, more giants were born from his legs and the sweat produced in his armpits.

The fires of Muspelheim and the frost of Niflheim continued their exchange and a cow known as Audhumla came forth to nourish Ymir with her milk. She was, in turn, sustained by licking the salty crystals of the ice. Licking away at these ice crystals, she soon wore them away, and Buri was revealed. He was the first of the Aesir gods to be created.

Buri was blessed with a son named Bor who wedded the giant Bolthorn's daughter Bestla. From this union came three giant half-god and half-giant sons. These sons were Odin, who later became the ruler of the gods, and his brothers Vili and Vé.

Seeing that Ymir and his ever-increasing family of frost giants were evil and cruel, Odin and his brothers planned to kill him. When they succeeded, they dragged his body to the center of the great void and created the world (one of the Nine Realms) from his corpse. Specifically, his blood became the sea and lakes, his flesh the earth, his hair grew into trees, and his bones shaped the mountains. The sky was made from his massive skull, and this was upheld for all eternity by four dwarves who represented the cardinal points.

As Ymir's flesh rotted, it filled with maggots, which the gods gifted with human insight and they gave to them the appearance of men. However, these were not men but dwarves, and they dwelled in the earth or hid in the rocks. The first four dwarves were Nordi, Vestri, Sundri, and Austri (north, west, south, and east), and they upheld the skull of Ymir. These dwarves also created magical weapons for the Aesir, including Thor's hammer Mjöllnir.

Ymir's brains became the clouds. With Ymir's death, a massive deluge of blood was released that washed most of the frost giants away, with only a few remaining.

The three godly brothers observed all that had happened, and sensing that the remaining Jötnar, two giants Bergelmir and his wife (and their offspring), would always threaten the new world, they made a protective wall (from Ymir's eyebrows) to safeguard this new land, which they called Midgard.

The word Midgard is loosely translated as "middle yard" or "middle earth," a term that has so been ingrained in mythology that it even appears in the story of *The Lord of The Rings* many centuries later. The reasoning behind the Norse use of Midgard is that since this new realm was halfway down the World Tree's trunk, it was suitable to call it thus. It also located earth as the center of the World Tree cosmos.

Finally, the three gods decided to create the first man and the first woman, Ask and Embla. Suitably, they made them from two tree trunks. Ask was made from an ash tree trunk and Embla from an elm trunk, although some legends indicate they were born from the Ymir's sweat, like the giants.

Other elements of the Norse creation myth are equally fascinating:

The Sun and the Moon

One man on Midgard was so arrogant and self-obsessed by the birth of his two beautiful children that he named them Mani and Sol (moon and sun), which angered the gods.

As punishment, the gods placed Sol (the girl) into a chariot (the sun) that rushes through the heavens. The chariot is drawn by two magical horses, Árvakr (early awake) and Alsviðr (very quick). The earth was shielded from the sun's fire by a shield strapped to the bottom of this stellar chariot.

The beautiful son, Mani, was forced to rush across the heavens in a chariot drawn by one horse Aldsvider, with two wolves called Sköll (treachery) and Hati (hate) chasing him. The wolves would bite him (giving the moon it's carved shape), but each month he would heal again.

Asgard

When Midgard had been formed, the three gods decided to create a world of their own, Asgard. They built this world high over Midgard, and the two worlds (and later the other worlds too) became joined by a rainbow bridge known as the Bifröst. Within Asgard, there are many realms, each belonging to different gods or goddesses.

The golden hall, Valhalla, is ruled by Odin and receives the souls of warriors slain honorably on the battlefield.

Himinbjörg is the realm ruled by Heimdallr who guards the entrance to the Bifröst. While there are other realms within Asgard; however, these two are important as they contribute specifically to the creation and Armageddon beliefs of Norse mythology.

When picturing what Asgard looked like, it is interesting to remember that it was the Viking idea of "heaven." Thus, it would have been a place of great beauty. There would have been great mountains, glittering oceans, magnificent sunsets, tall forests, and of course, the different halls of the gods, which were each more majestic than the rest.

The Nine Realms

Among the Germanic tribes, the numbers nine and three are quite auspicious. Throughout their mythology, we encounter these numbers. With the nine worlds along the World Tree, we find but the first instance of the number nine. These nine worlds or realms are Niflheim, Muspelheim, Asgard, Midgard, Vanaheim, Alfheim, Jotunheim, Svartalfheim, and lastly, Helheim.

Niflheim and Muspelheim had been made out of the great void, but the other realms were all made from Ymir's body. A closer look at each of the Nine Realms provides an interesting look at the mythological views of the Norse people.

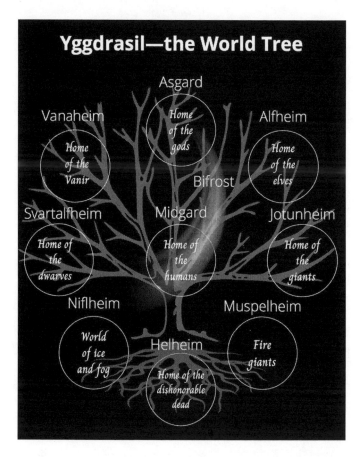

Image 6: Russo self-designed image. Diagrammatic representation of the World Tree with the Nine Realms and the conditions or inhabitants of each shown.

- **Niflheim**

Meaning: World of Fog

One of the oldest realms or worlds of the World Tree, Niflheim is a cold and dark region. It contains the oldest spring, Hvergelmir, which is protected by a fearsome dragon called Nidhug. From this fountain comes the 11 rivers that feed energy to the rest of the universe. All the living energies or people will eventually return to this fountain. Not much is known about the landscape of Niflheim, but it is assumed to be a frozen world since the ice giants or ice energy came from there.

- **Muspelheim**

Meaning: The World of Múspell

Ancestral home of the fire giants and polar opposite to Niflheim in the north. This is a place of fire, lava, ash, sparks, and soot. The sparks from Muspelheim are rumored to have been the first stars. Home to the fire giants and demons, its landscape is loosely equivalent to the Christian idea of hell.

The ruler of Muspelheim is a savage giant known as Sutr or Múspell. His destiny is to attack Asgard during the end of days of Ragnarok. True to myth, this ending of the world through the actions and attacks of Sutr will be in the form of fire. It is through his doing that Asgard will burn.

- **Asgard**

Meaning: Enclosure of the Aesir

The fortified home of the gods and goddesses, located in the middle of the World Tree, high above Midgard. This is the epitome of order and justice, while the home of the frost giants is the antithesis of this, being made up of chaos and injustice. The human world, Midgard, tried to emulate the world of the gods, basing their laws on the divine ones.

Valhalla is located in Asgard, and this is where fallen warriors go, making Asgard the concept of heaven to the Norsemen and women. It is a golden hall that is under the authority of Odin, the Allfather.

During Ragnarok, Asgard is destroyed in fire, and many of the gods perish along with it. However, after the destruction of the old world, a new Asgard is said to arise, and this is one that is wealthier and more magnificent than before. In Christian terms, this is the new Jerusalem concept of heaven being recreated for all humans.

- **Midgard**

Meaning: Middle enclosure

This is the world or earth created from Ymir's body, and it is the concept of civilization. It is also where the humans live. For the ancient Norse or Vikings, their world was made up of land surrounded by dangerous seas with "monsters" such as storms, sharks, and whales that destroyed their ships and threatened their communities. To represent this, they created the mythology that Midgard was surrounded by hostile seas with giants and other creatures (Jotunheim) that threatened the humans of Midgard. These hostile lands that surrounded the earth were represented by Jotunheim, the home of the frost giants and the symbol of chaos.

Image 7: Image by Jonas Friese on Unsplash. The fearsome creatures that small wooden vessels had to face in the world's oceans may have inspired the mythic creatures that threatened Midgard.

The main creature that threatened Midgard was Jormungand, a terrifying serpent that lived in the seas of chaos around Midgard. During the end time or Ragnarok, the world Midgard sinks beneath the ocean of blood. It drowns in the massive waves that the great serpent makes as it writhes in the waters surrounding Midgard.

- **Jotunheim**

Meaning: World of the Giants

The feared frost giants live here, and these are the sworn enemies of the gods and of men. Mostly, this land is rough and barren with occasionally dense and impenetrable forests and abandoned frozen regions on the ocean shores. In terms of earth's geography, this might have been the Greenland and the North Pole, which was frightening to the Norse sailors to behold.

According to myth, the giants have no society of their own, and in the chaos, they live off what they can find such as fish, deer, and birds from the ocean and forests. The giants have their own version of Asgard called the stronghold of Utgard. This is carved from blocks of snow and ice. The giants hunger for the days of Ragnarok, and they wish to storm forth and swamp civilization, spreading their chaos to the rest of the World Tree.

- **Vanaheim**

Meaning: Homeland of the Vanir

This world is home to the Vanir gods who are more nature spirits than the newer Asgard gods. These gods have powers over fertility, health, and other forms of sorcery. The only Vanir who are mentioned in Norse mythology are Njord, Freya, and Freyr. These gods are like the Greek muses, and through their magic, they can see the future and mold it, but never change it. They predict that Ragnarok will see the destruction of Asgard and the other worlds.

- **Alfheim**

Meaning: Homeland of the Elves

Situated next to Asgard, this is the world of light bringers or angels. This world is ruled by the god Freyr, and these elves or angels have power over nature and fertility and are known to inspire the poets or bards. Given the warrior mentality of the early Norsemen, Alfheim doesn't feature strongly in the myths, although many records from that time may be lost due to the oral traditions not always having been recorded on parchment with the later influence of Latin scholars.

- **Svartalfheim/Nidavellir**

Meaning: The Dark Fields or Home of the Black Elves

When the maggots that formed in Ymir's body were turned into dwarves, this is where they moved to. The dwarves, who were also referred to as the black elves, lived here among the rocks and in caves. This would probably have been an extensive system of subterranean caves and caverns where the dwarves had mines, forges, and workshops. The dwarves were master craftsmen, and they were rumored to have forged many of the Asgardian gods' weapons such as Thor's hammer and Odin's spear. They also created the fabled chain that finally bound Fenrir in a last attempt to stave off Ragnarok.

- **Helheim**

Meaning: Hel's home

Loosely, this is hell since it is where the dishonorable dead are sent. Though, this world is not anything like the Christian idea of hell. This world is ruled by Loki's daughter, Hel. Those who die without honor are sent to this place to spend eternity. This army of miscreants will become Hel's weapon against the other gods during Ragnarok.

The Major Gods

The gods that feature in Norse mythology include groups of deities and individual gods or goddesses too. Each is a unique character with their own personality and characteristics, which makes Norse mythology truly interesting.

The name Aesir is the collective noun for the gods who lived in Asgard. Also, the Aesir mythical gods of war and sky included Odin, Thor, Tyr, Loki, Baldur, and other gods too. Initially, the Aesir gods and the Vanir gods made war upon each other, fighting for dominance, but eventually, they reached a peaceful accord, living in relative peace on the World Tree.

In a move toward a more amicable relationship between the Aesir and Vanir, prisoners were exchanged between the two sides to keep the peace. This may have explained the similar practice among the Norse tribes where conflict was ended with the exchange of prisoners to keep a peaceful relationship going.

Living in Vanaheim, the Vanir were believed to have power over the earth, prosperity, and fertility. The gods Njord and his children Freyr and Freyja were known to be of the Vanir. They were sent to the Aesir gods as an exchange to preserve peace. Due to the prisoner exchanges, the two sides later united and would fight together against the giants during Ragnarok.

The Aesir sent Hönir and Mimir as exchange for Njord, Freyr, and Freyja. However, legend has it that when the Vanir noticed how Hönir looked to Mimir for guidance, they beheaded Mimir out of vengeance. Odin didn't declare war in return for the affront, choosing instead to preserve Mimir's head with a magic ritual and placed it over the fountain of wisdom below Yggdrasil.

What has been pointed out is that the exchange of prisoners brought great things to Asgard, with Freyja possibly marrying Odin and becoming his wife (Skjalden, 2020). Though there is some ambiguity in this regard as this implies she was Frigg as well as being Freya. In Norse Mythology, there is often some interchange between similar gods. Perhaps this is due to different tribes telling the same story but with subtle changes. Freya also taught Odin magic, since she was believed to have been a sorceress and the goddess of love.

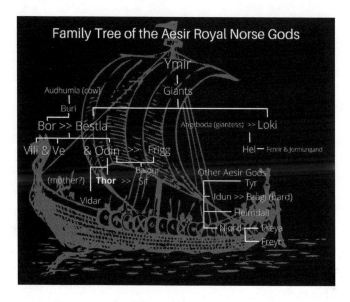

Image 8: Russo self-designed image. The gods of Asgard were mostly descended from the royal lineage of Odin's family; however, some were descended from giants like Loki.

- **Ymir**

Ymir (also called Aurgelmir) was technically not a god. It was the ancestor of the giants, and it had terrible powers. Therefore, we can consider it a deity too.

Ymir was the first creature to be created in the Norse mythology. It formed in Ginnungagap. From its death at the hands of Odin and his brothers, Ymir's body became the world. In a sense, we can consider Ymir to be the creation act or raw energy that the world was shaped out of.

- **Odin**

Eldest son of Bor and Bestla, Odin is known as the "Allfather" or the "father of battle." The character of Odin is complex and filled with dualities. While he is fearsome and unforgiving, he is also wise and all-knowing. He was the god of poetry and war, wisdom and death. He, in turn, fathered Thor and Baldur, among some other lesser known gods.

Odin was the patron of kings and bandits alike, again showing his duality of nature. While he favored stern governance, he had little time for laws. His very name meant "master of all." And while Odin could be the life of the party with his friends, he was a terrifying sight to behold on the battlefield. His characteristics were often ascribed to fearsome Nordic warriors or berserkers who lost all sense during battle and fought without any awareness of injuries.

Being born of a mother who was a giant, Odin was different from the other gods. He was also known to be both Asgardian and Vanirian. With Odin, nothing was simple or straightforward. He was many things. We'll dive into more detail on the enigmatic and multi-layered Odin in Chapter 3.

- **Vili and Vé**

Odin's two brothers represent the other sides of the creation diad, "Inspiration, Conscious Intention, and the Sacred" (McCoy, n.d.-d). The two brothers killed the giant Ymir with Odin, and they created the world from the giant's body. There are also other myths involving these two brothers, and they were prominent figures in early Germanic mythological beliefs.

One other mention of them in the *Poetic Edda* is when Odin was banned from Asgard for practicing forms of magic that were considered "unmanly." The two brothers allegedly slept with Odin's wife Frigg while he was away, which, if true, might question the parentage of at least one of Odin's children.

- **Frigg**

Frigg or sometimes Frigga was Odin's wife and mother of Baldur. In literature, Frigg is sometimes used interchangeably with Friya, and at other times, they are two distinct goddesses. Frigg is shown as using Norse magic, which is known as seidr.

She had many magical skills that were depicted in her ability to weave, her shapeshifting into the form of a falcon (which she kept feathers for), and her ability to know the future. In mythology, Freya had a husband, who is essentially Odin. This implied the two goddesses shared Odin as husband.

- **Thor**

The oldest son of Odin, Thor's name means "thunder." Most of the Germanic tribes worshiped Thor before their conversion to Christianity. With his representation as a noble, honorable, and physically superior god of war, he was well liked and respected by the Norse tribes. Thor was the tireless defender of Asgard from the chaos of the giants. His most famous possession was the hammer, Mjöllnir, which represented lightning.

Yet, Thor also owned several other weapons and treasures that were spectacular. He had a pair of steel gloves that were specially made so he could handle the magnificent Mjöllnir, which could fly through the air with tremendous speed. These gloves, called Járngreipr (meaning: iron grippers), allowed Thor to catch the hammer as it returned to him when he threw it.

While Thor was powerful and physically superior to any of the other gods, he also had a magical belt called Megingjörd (meaning: belt of power) that doubled his incredible strength. To say that facing Thor was an intimidating prospect was certainly an understatement.

Thor's nemesis is the great serpent, Jormungand, which he fights against during Ragnarok. Here, Thor and the serpent slay each other though legend has it that Thor revives himself again after the battle.

The claim is that Thor's mother was a giant, and since Odin was half-giant, that meant Thor supposedly was a "three-quarter giant." Thor had a particular relationship with the humans of Midgard who often appealed to him for aid. Nordic tribes asked Thor to bless their land and marriages as well as guide them in battle.

Thor is said to be married to a little-known goddess called Sif, whose golden hair was representative of grain or harvests.

- **Baldur**

Odin's son from his wife Frigg, Baldur loosely means "bold." However, he was more than just bold. He was said to be so cheerful that he gave off light. Baldur was the god of light and purity. In most of the literature, Baldur is portrayed as being mild and pleasant, but there is evidence that Baldur was as fierce a warrior as his half-brother Thor. Most of the myth surrounding Baldur concerns his death and the visions he had, as well as a magical journey to try and rescue him from death.

- **Vidar**

Known only as a distant son of Odin, Vidar's claim to mythological fame is that he survived Ragnarok and was the god who slew the great wolf Fenrir once it had killed and devoured Odin. He is involved in Norse religious practices, and at least two places in Norway are named after him: Virsu (meaning: temple of Vidar) and Viskjøl (meaning: rocky outcropping of Vidar). Due to his role as the Slayer of Fenrir in retaliation for the wolf's slaying of Odin, he is known as the god of vengeance.

- **Tyr**

Known primarily as the god of justice and law, Tyr is remembered today still in the naming of Tuesday (Tyr's day). He was one of the most dominant Norse gods in the early Viking era. In the *Poetic Edda*, the Valkyrie Sigrdrifa tells the human hero Sigurd to ask for Tyr's blessings before battle (McCoy, n.d.-c).

- **Bragi**

Some Norse myth and later translations of documents from the later Viking era held Bragi to be a Norse god when he was reported to have been a human bard or poet. He was so popular in life that he was believed to have been made a god in death by Odin to entertain and regal the fallen warriors who traveled to Odin's hall (Valhalla) upon their deaths. Later, he was believed to be the god of poetry, which is unlikely as Odin drank the mead of poetry and was known as the god of poetry too.

- **Idun**

Wife to Bragi, Idun was the keeper of the fruits of immortality. Her fruits were said to sustain the immortal gods, and she is mostly known to appear in the story of the kidnapping of Idun, where she was said to have been kidnapped by Loki.

- **Sif**

Wife to Thor, there is little mention of her in the *Poetic Edda,* other than the incident when Loki, the trickster, cut off her hair, which resulted in Loki having to approach the dwarves to make her a head of golden hair and Thor's hammer too.

Sif was said to be a goddess of fertility or the harvest, and this makes sense in ancient Norse beliefs where Thor was the lightning god, who fertilizes the earth, creating a perfect union of this marriage.

- **Hermod**

Another distant son of Odin, this god is mostly known as the god who rode Sleipnir to the underworld to plead for Baldur's release. Other passing references to Hermod have him welcoming fallen warriors to Odin's hall and receiving armor as a blessing from the Allfather. Like many of the other Asgardian gods, he was also known to have occasional interactions with the humans of Midgard.

- **Loki**

Known as the trickster, Loki features prominently in Norse mythology. He is often an ambiguous figure in mythical tales, and his actions rarely serve in the best interest of the gods. When Loki is involved, he will always do what is right for him.

His father was the giant Farbauti (meaning: cruel striker) and his mother was the giantess Laufey. Loki had a daughter, Hel, by the giantess Angrboda (meaning: anguish boden), who had an assortment of vile creatures at her bidding to inflict all manner of painful injuries upon the other gods. One of these, the wolf Fenrir, even killed Odin during Ragnarok.

- **Hel**

Daughter to Loki, Hel ruled the underworld (also called Hel). While little is known of Hel, the poet Snorri referred to her as being half black and half white, and he wrote that she had a fierce and terrifying expression on her face. She was said to be the sister of the great wolf, Fenrir, and the serpent, Jormungand.

- **Heimdall**

One of the better known Aesir gods, Heimdall is known to be the guardian of Asgard and specifically the Bifröst. He was characterized as being a fearsome warrior with exceptional powers of hearing and sight, and he could see enemies approach from miles away and hear the grass grow. He sat at the entrance to the Bifröst with the great horn Gjallarhorn, which he blew upon when enemies of Asgard drew near. The greatest of these events that caused him to blow the horn in warning is the start of Ragnarok.

While Heimdall is the loyal and ordered god of Asgard, Loki is the trickster who will betray him. During Ragnarok, the two will slay each other. Heimdall's birth is somewhat mystical and makes for an exciting tale, which I'll share in Chapter 4.

- **Njord**

One of the most powerful Vanir gods was Njord, who was sent to Asgard during the Asgard-Vanir war as a prisoner along with his two children, Freyr and Freya. Njord was the god of the sea and prosperity.

- **Freyr**

Son of Njord, Freyr was also sent to Asgard to secure peace between the Asgardians and the Vanir after their war. He is venerated as the god of fertility, and he was often invoked at marriages and harvest festivals. Traditionally, he is shown with his totemic animal, a huge boar, and a massive erect phallus. He was also reputed to have been sexually involved with many goddesses and even giantesses, including his own sister, Freya. The Vanir seemed to have had little problem with incestuous deeds among their gods.

Being associated with festivity and prosperity, Freyr was well liked among the early Germanic tribes. He is also said to have been instrumental in the origins of many tribes and royal lines.

- **Freya**

Daughter of Njord, she is later also said to have been married to Odin. She is renowned to be the goddess of fate and destiny. Freya was sent as prisoner to Asgard with her father Njord and brother Freyr. She is, therefore, considered both a Vanir and Aesir goddess.

- **Sigyn**

The wife of Loki, this Asgardian goddess features in several tales about Loki. Not to be confused with the giantess Loki sired Hel, Jormungand, and Fenrir with, Sigyn is the mother of Loki's two Asgardian children, Vali and Narfi.

The Giants

There are many giants mentioned throughout Norse mythology, and several of these possessed powers akin to those of the gods. Their influence on the gods and presence in the tales of Norse mythology make them an unmissable component to the worlds of Yggdrasil. Here are a few of the prominent giants who feature in mythology:

- **Skadi**

While many of the giants were portrayed as being violent and aggressive towards man and gods, Skadi was associated with winter. She was known as a more benevolent giantess. While she had been married to Njord, a god of the Vanir, her union didn't last as she preferred icy weather, while he preferred beach landscapes and mild weather.

- **Surt**

This fiery giant is quite important as he is the commander of the army of giants that descends on Asgard during Ragnarok. The fiery sword of Surt could also have been the volcanic eruptions that characterized Iceland during that historic era.

- **Aegir and Ran**

These two giants were known to live under the ocean, and they were attributed with generous spirits and divine culinary skills. They often socialized with the Asgardians, and they participated in cooking for the gods and making mead for Odin's feasts.

While there were many other giants also mentioned in the *Poetic Edda*, these are better known and had more unique characteristics that are worth noting.

Other Creatures

The worlds of Yggdrasil were also populated by a mix of strange creatures other than the gods, giants, and men. The world of Svartalfheim was populated by the dwarves (or black elves), while the world of Alfheim was home to the elves. These creatures also featured in a supporting capacity in most of the mythological tales of the Norse gods. In addition to these two races, there were also other beings that feature in mythology that are ambiguous in their origin but are worth mentioning nonetheless.

- **The Elves**

The Vanir seemed to have a particular bond with the elves who were described as being light and made of light. Freyr, a Vanir god, was noted as being the lord of the elven homeworld Alfheim. With the Vanir gods being associated with harvest, nature, and fertility, it is no stretch to assume the elves shared these characteristics.

Humans and elves had a strange relationship according to myth, with the elves both causing and healing diseases among the humans, and instances of interbreeding were strongly hinted at. The Norse peoples were known to venerate the elves for centuries after their conversion to Christianity and the lapsing of the worship of the Norse gods.

- **The Dwarves**

According to Norse myth, the dwarves were formed from worms that burrowed from Ymir's flesh after his death. They were black in color and were renowned as miners, craftsmen, and also magicians. Dwarves also had to live underground as sunlight supposedly turned them to stone.

- **Mimir**

The shadowy being who guards the well of wisdom (the Well of Urd), Mimir is a wise and steadfast counselor who guides the gods. He was savagely beheaded during the Asgard-Vanir war, but Odin kept his head, using magic to preserve life and wisdom in the appendage. There are instances when Mimir's head counseled Odin during great tribulations.

- **Kvasir**

While not a creature as such, Kvasir was a magical human who was made from mead brewed at the end of the Asgard-Vanir war. All the gods had chewed berries and spat these into a vat to be fermented. This mead turned into the human Kvasir, who possessed wisdom to know the answer to all questions.

Kvasir deserves mention since his death produces a mead that could turn anyone who drank it into a poet or scholar. This is also an interesting tale involving Odin on another of his quests to gain wisdom. But I'll share this interesting tale in the next chapter.

- **Völva**

The Völva was a long dead seeress or witch who dwelled in Helheim. Using seidr magic, the Völva could perceive the future, and she could tell what would happen. Baldur's death was predicted by the Völva, leaving Odin in much grief. Following Völva's prediction, Frigg set out to find a way to save her son's life.

- **The Norns**

These magical beings were responsible for fate. While they were hardly imposing women, these female beings determined what would happen to every living being in the cosmos. There were three Norns: Urd (meaning: past), Verdandi (meaning: what is being shaped right now), and Skuld (meaning: what will be).

The Norns had several fate-making rituals or tasks they used to decide what would happen in the present, the past, and the future. Likely, each of the Norns were predisposed to the time-aspect corresponding with their names. To decide fate, they would use wooden lots, create a magically woven cloth (as destiny unravels), or carve rune symbols into wood, such as with the carving of the runes into the trunk of Yggdrasil when Odin learned to read the runes. The Norns were simply fate creators, and they did so in a completely impartial way. The ancient Norse didn't worship them, and while they didn't fear them, they respected their powers.

- **Valkyrie**

These female spirits (meaning: choosers of the fallen) were Odin's helpers to choose fallen heroes from the battlefield. Once a hero had been chosen by a Valkyrie, they would bear him on their wings to Odin's hall, Valhalla. While some texts promoted the Valkyrie as being noble spirits, others suggest the Valkyrie chose the slain *before* the battle, thereby *causing* death.

In the "Darraðarljóð," a poem from Njal's Saga, the Valkyrie are portrayed as grotesque spirits who weave a dark magic using a weaving loom, intestines, skulls, and terrifying enjoyment as they plot which warriors would live and which would die.

- **Hugin and Munin**

The two ravens are often seen with Odin, and they assist him with gathering information about what is happening in the cosmos, and they assist his spirit helpers by carrying his orders and returning with updates on how things were with the realms of Yggdrasil.

Their names were so interlinked in meaning, they are commonly just known as "thought and memory." In Norse traditions, they were seen as a blessing whenever a blood sacrifice was made to Odin, as seeing ravens circle the freshly slaughtered animal offering was a sign that Odin had accepted the offering. Like Odin, the ravens are intelligent and they are also fierce fighters, showing Odin's dualistic character through these familiar animals.

Hugin is most often referred to, and Norsemen would use a kind of literary device almost like personification by referring to warriors as the ones who redden Hugin's beak or drown the field in Hugin's blood.

- **Einherjar**

The best soldiers and warriors who fell in battle were chosen by the Valkyrie and taken to Odin's fabled golden hall known as Valhalla. There they were trained daily to become part of his Einherjar, which is a host of warriors who would fight with Odin during Ragnarok. These warriors enjoyed an exemplary life as Vikings, fighting by day, feasting by night, and come the morning, all their wounds would be completely healed. The feasts came from magical sources too, with the meat being from the Saehrimnir, a boar who was slaughtered for the warriors, but was then reborn the next day, only to be slaughtered again. The mead was from the goat Heidrun, and every night, the warriors could drink all the mead they could milk from its udder. In the morning, the goat's udder would be filled with mead again.

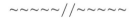

The gods and goddesses of Norse mythology are often interconnected in strange familial relationships, making for conflict-rich events. Represented in myths and tales, we can learn more about their character and powers through the stories they feature in. Each tale is an opportunity not only for learning about Norse beliefs but also for reflecting on our own in the modern world we live in. The Aesir royal family were certainly involved in an assortment of strange, terrifying, and even humorous tales.

Chapter 4:

The Royal Family

Image 9: Victor B on Unsplash. The Viking myths and tales were often depictions of massive battles, conflicts, war, and victories or losses. As a warrior culture, courage was proven in sacrifice. Odin's sacrifices rank chief among these.

Odin

Odin has much the appearance as the modern representation of Gandalf the Gray from *the Lord of the Rings* movies, and he appears as an old man with a long white beard and one missing eye. He is shown in ancient illustrations as wearing a cloak and a hood with his spear Gungnir in his hand. Sometimes, he travels with his wolves Geri and Freki as well as his two ravens.

Odin's triple horn, which was made from three interlocking mead horns also appears in Norse mythology. The mead horn had great importance in Norse traditions where it was used to toast during feasts.

Being all-seeing, Odin traveled the land, but his two ravens Hugin and Munin (meaning: thought and memory) would soar through the skies of Midgard and report all they saw in the realm of men to Odin.

Unlike modern depictions of Odin as being a benevolent ruler, he was historically noted as being a warmonger, inciting violence and conflict among tribes (McCoy, n.d.-b). Other war gods like Thor were seen as being much more noble of character. Odin's totemic representation is usually as a bear or wolf. All of the warriors who swore affiliation to these enjoyed Odin's patronage. He favored strong-willed people, but mostly warriors and kings or outlaws. Average people were of little interest to Odin.

Odin was always questing for more knowledge or magic, and he would take extreme measures to attain this, even going as far as to sacrifice an eye to gain knowledge from the fountain of wisdom. In another legend, Odin performed a self-sacrifice by hanging on the World Tree or Yggdrasil for nine days and nights to gain magical insight into the writing system of the Norse, the Germanic runes, or alphabet.

Known to undertake shamanic journeys, Odin practiced advanced magic and was known to enter a deep sleep state known as Odinsleep where he gained magical insight.

Image 10: Russo self-designed image. Odin, the Allfather, is a prominent figure in many tales and myths from Norse mythology. He was both wise and fearsome.

Odin's Quest for Wisdom

Odin was so obsessed with wisdom that he was willing to make any sacrifice to gain it. When he learned of the Well of Urd at the roots of Yggdrasil (as per the

"Völuspá"), he journeyed down to the twisted roots, hoping to gain knowledge and wisdom from the well. The waters of the well contained wisdom, and those who drank from the well would be imbued with wisdom and great knowledge.

However, the Well of Urd was guarded by a shadowy figure known as Mimir, which prevented all from drinking from the well. Odin stopped and asked the guardian for a drink of water from the well as he was so thirsty from his journey. Mimir refused, saying that those who wished to drink from the well would have to sacrifice an eye first. Having seen how passionately Odin wanted the waters of the well, Mimir had decided that Odin could drink of the waters and sate his thirst for knowledge if he made a great enough sacrifice to earn the valuable reward of wisdom. Hence, Odin had to choose between sacrificing his own eye for the right to drink the waters of wisdom. Odin bravely plucked out his own eye to seal the deal. Mimir, honoring their deal, dipped his horn or cup into the well and offered Odin a drink.

While Odin left the well with only one eye, he had gained much wisdom. It is unclear what wisdom Odin gained in exchange for his eye, but it is believed that many of his following quests and visions were based on his hard-earned insights. This story of self-sacrifice may have been a parable that reflected on the concept that losing some of your earthly vision (represented by an eye) in exchange for wisdom (personal insight) is a wise deal.

Odin and the Mead of Poetry

Kvasir, who was created out of the mead brewed after the Asgard-Vanir war, was slain by two dwarves. He had been traveling the land, dispensing wisdom to all, and the dwarves, greedy to possess his power, slew him, making mead from the man's blood.

This mead gave all who drank it the ability to act with wisdom. Of course, this was a gift the gods desired, especially Odin, who was constantly questing for greater wisdom. It was said that drinking this mead could give you wisdom and make you either a poet or a scholar.

The gods soon tracked Kvasir's path, and finding the dwarves who had seen him last, they wanted to know what had happened, to which the dwarves lied, saying Kvasir had choked on his own wisdom.

These two dwarves had developed a taste for killing immortal and magical beings, and they set out to kill the giant Gilling by drowning him in the ocean. When his wife cried and lamented too loudly, the dwarves also killed her. However, this earned them the wrath of Gilling's son, Suttung, who took the two dwarves to a shallow reef as the tide was changing, threatening to drown them. As it goes with these tales, the giant was swayed from his vengeance by the offer of treasure. In this case, the treasure was the mead made from Kvasir's blood.

Letting them go in exchange for every last drop of the special mead, Suttung hid the mead in a mountain fortress where his daughter guarded it.

Enter Odin.

Hearing of the mead being hidden away, Odin decided he had to find out where. So, he set off in disguise (which was Odin's way), traveling to Suttung's brother's farm. There Odin deceived the nine farm hands, who worked for Baugi (Suttung's brother). He tricked them into killing each other, leaving Baugi without labor for the season.

Odin (in disguise as a lowly farm hand) offered to work for Baugi, bringing in the harvest by doing the work of nine men. In exchange, Odin asked for a sip of Suttung's magical mead. Baugi said it wasn't really up to him as Suttung was jealously guarding his mead, but he agreed to help Odin find it.

Bringing in a harvest when you have the skills of magic and godly strength is hardly an issue, and Odin easily brought in the harvest, claiming his reward from Baugi, who took him to see Suttung. However, Suttung refused to give a mere farm hand even one sip of his mead. So, Odin pleaded with Baugi to take him as close to the mead as he could, which Baugi did.

Standing next to a rock face that joined onto the chamber where Suttung's daughter guarded the mead, Odin took out an auger (a drill called Rati) and instructed Baugi to drill a hole into the chamber. Baugi tried to deceive Odin by only drilling halfway, but when Odin blew into the hole and the dust blew back into his face, he knew the hole wasn't complete, so he asked Baugi to drill further. Finally, satisfied that he could blow the dust into the chamber beyond, Odin quickly changed into a snake and sped through the hole.

Realizing who the farm hand was, Baugi tried to stab the snake with the auger, but Odin made it into the chamber where he seduced the giantess into giving him the mead. In exchange for sleeping with her for three nights, Odin drank all three casks that contained the mead, draining them to the dredges.

Odin then changed into an eagle, and with the mead in his stomach, he flew back to Asgard. The giant Suttung also changed into an eagle and flew after Odin, but in typical Norse style, Odin reached Asgard in the nick of time.

Taking wooden vats, Odin then regurgitated the mead into them, and this mead was shared among the gods Odin felt were worthy of it. In a comical twist, a few drops of the mead fell from Odin-eagle's beak, trickling down to Midgard, which accounts for all the bad poets and ill-informed scholars on earth. Those who had real talent in poetry and prose were gifted by Odin himself and not those last few drops.

Odin's Learning of the Runes

On another quest, Odin learned that the trunk of Yggdrasil, which grows from the well of Urd, had been carved with runes by three maidens known as the Norns. What the Norns carved in the tree affected all nine of the realms of Yggdrasil. Anyone who could read these runes were then able to see all nine the realms of Yggdrasil. These realms were normally invisible to the eye.

The runes were more than just an alphabet. Rather, they held great cosmological value and were closely connected to the power of control over the forces of life and magic. Being able to read the runes imbued the reader with great power and insights that far exceeded their contemporaries. Odin's search for the knowledge to read the runes was about his quest to control magic.

Again, to acquire this powerful gift, Odin was required to make a sacrifice, which enabled him to "earn" the knowledge to read the runes. As an act of self-sacrifice, Odin hung upon the tree of Yggdrasil by impaling himself on his spear, Gungnir. For nine days and nine nights Odin hung from the tree, dying a little each day. He stared into the waters of the well, refusing help from any other gods as he bore the terrible pain in stoic silence.

On the ninth night, Odin's mind opened and he learned the knowledge and wisdom to read the runes. This gave him great wisdom, and he could cure the sick, nullify the weapons of his attackers, and make women love him. Perhaps this is also where he gained the knowledge of what was fated to happen during Ragnarok. There is little chronological order to Odin's mythical journeys and quests, so we don't know if he gained this knowledge before building his golden hall and creating Valhalla so he might create his army of brave warriors who had fallen in battle. Was Odin preparing for the great and final conflict?

Image 11: Husein Bahr on Unsplash. Wife to Odin, Frigg was a great practitioner of magic.

Frigg

Odin's search for knowledge and wisdom culminated in his quests to understand magic. He often indulged in magical rites to gain wisdom despite this not being seemly for a man in Norse tradition. Odin's marriage to Frigg, which means beloved, may also not have been one of romance, but rather of convenience and valuable exchange. Frigg (or Freya according to some conflicting interpretations of the *Poetic Edda)* taught her magic to Odin.

Frigg was the queen of all goddesses and had power over love, fertility, the sky, motherhood, marriage, and other domestic aspects of the female psyche. As she was a fertility goddess, she was associated with the full moon.

The gods were often involved in the affairs of the men of the North (Norsemen). One instance is recorded of the Vandals and the Winnilers (two warring Germanic tribes) fighting each other and Frigg and Odin each choosing an opposing side. Wanting the conflict to stop spilling into their home, Odin swore to support whichever side he saw first thing in the morning. He knew he would see the Vandals first as his bedroom window faced that way.

Frigg was a talented strategist, and she cleverly told the women of the Winnilers tribe to place their long hats under their chins so they might look like long beards.

Then, while Odin slept, she turned their bed, so Odin would wake while facing towards the side of the Winniler tribe. When Odin awoke, he was confused by the long beards he was seeing. Odin knew Frigg had fooled him. Yet, he still kept his word and sided with the Winniler tribe, granting them victory (Geller, 2016).

Frigg and the Gift of Future Vision

Frigg and Freya, who was Njord's daughter, were both highly skilled in magic. On one occasion, Loki was crashing a party at Odin's hall. Being the god of trickery, Loki proceeded to taunt the gods, especially Frigg, whom he provoked by saying that he had been the one to decide that her son Baldur would never be released from Helheim again. Frigg was unable to respond to this, but Freya responded by warning Loki that teasing Frigg was not wise as Frigg had the gift of foresight and knew the fates of all men and gods. Thankfully for Loki, Frigga was prevented from speaking these fates aloud.

In the "Lokasenna," or Loki's Truth Game (North, 2010), a poem from the *Poetic Edda*, Loki confronts Frigg publicly. He accuses her of taking both Odin's brothers as lovers while Odin was away on one of his quests, and this is why Freya warned him to mind his manners or face a grim truth of the future.

While Frigg is mentioned frequently, she doesn't participate in any major quests or myths where she features dominantly. Her main claim to notoriety is being Odin's wife and mother to Baldur.

Image 12: Image by ANIRUDH on Unsplash. Today, one of the most widely recognized symbols and weapons of antiquity and myth is the hammer of Thor (Mjöllnir).

Thor

Unlike the Hollywood depiction of Thor as being a blonde giant with a square jaw, the Norse depiction of the god of thunder shows him to be a large red haired and bearded giant. His size was impressively large, and in most images, he more than dwarfs those around him.

Thor was a son of Odin, but his mother was not Frigg. Instead, it is reported that Thor's mother was a giantess, Jord, indicating the brutish physical power that Thor would have possessed. There are many myths and stories that are recounted in the *Poetic Edda* in which Thor features.

While Thor married a goddess named Sif, and he had three children, but only two with her, namely Thrud and Magni. His other son was Moi; his mother might have been a giantess but the information about this isn't conclusive. Thor represented the three pillars of manhood: procreation, protection, and providing. While Thor wasn't known for anything other than his ability to produce violence, he did protect those who needed him, and the gods and mortals were quick to summon him. He was a favorite god to call upon before battle, during marriage celebrations, and if you were facing an angry giant, like the gods did during the building of Asgard's wall (but more on that in Chapter 5).

Thor's magical hammer, Mjöllnir, features prominently in his tales. It brought lightning when he struck the ground, and he could pulverize both gods, giants, and creatures with it. The hammer was supposed to be passed down to one of Thor's sons in true Nordic tradition, though this did not happen due to the events of Ragnarok.

With his characteristics of being quick to act, being rash, having nobility of spirit, and protecting others, Thor was the archetypal warrior that Norsemen tried to aspire to.

The Feast and Killing of Hrungnir

This fable perfectly portrays Thor's commitment to family. Odin had been riding his magnificent stallion Sleipnir through the countryside. Meeting the giant Hrungnir (also on a horse) along the way, a race ensued. With eight legs, Sleipnir easily won the race back to Asgard. The giant and Odin were quite civil to each other, and Odin invited Hrungnir to stay for a feast that night.

During the feast, Hrungnir gorged himself and drank barrels of mead, soon becoming quite drunk. He looked around, noticing the many beautiful goddesses that were present at the feast, and in a boastful tone, he said, "I will destroy Asgard, but not before I have claimed each of the goddesses here as my concubines!" Roaring with laughter, the giant continued to leer at the goddesses, including Sif, Thor's Aesir wife.

As honor dictated, Thor quickly challenged the giant to a fight, and the drunken giant instantly sobered a bit when he beheld the sheer size of Thor. Quickly, he agreed to the fight but only if they could meet in Jotunheim where his weapons were. This was quite a journey, and Hrungnir sent word ahead to the other giants that they might devise a clever plan to slay the god.

They constructed a clay figure that was 30 miles high and 10 miles in breadth. And it was this juggernaut figure whom they hoped would slay Thor. However, the clay golem offered no real challenge to Thor and his mighty hammer. When it saw Thor, the clay giant ran.

When Thor threw his hammer, Hrungnir hurled a whetstone with his slingshot at Thor. Mjöllnir passed through the clay figure, shattering it, and it passed on to crush the giant's head. The whetstone lodged in Thor's head, and rumor had it that the whetstone was lodged in Thor's skull until Ragnarok.

The Making of Thor's Hammer

Loki, being a great mischief-maker, had cut the golden hair from Sif's head. Thor, her husband, was enraged and he was about to smite Loki when Loki claimed that he could go to Svartalfheim, the home of the black elves or dwarves, and instruct them in how to make a new head of hair for Sif.

Ever the silver-tongued devil, Loki convinced Thor who allowed him to journey to the mines of

Svartalfheim. A dwarf, Ivaldi, had his two sons make the head of golden hair for Loki as well as two other treasures that he sent back to Asgard. These treasures were Odin's spear (Gungnir) and a marvelous ship (Skidbladnir), which could be folded up small enough to fit into your pocket.

However, Loki was far from done trickering around on Svartalfheim, and he challenged the dwarven brothers Brokkr and Sindri to make better and more advanced crafted items than the spear and the magical ship. Overcome by jealousy, the dwarves worked tirelessly, crafting their magical objects. The first was a golden boar (Gullinbursti), which gave off light with its golden bristles. And the second item was a wonderful and magical ring (Draupnir), from which eight golden rings dripped every nine nights.

Finally, the dwarf brothers made a very powerful and costly gift. It was the pinnacle of their creations, but they had to focus and pay strict attention. However, Loki, being devious, changed into a fly and bit Brokkr's eyelid, causing blood to run into his eyes, distracting the dwarf from his work. The work the dwarves made was truly spectacular. They had made a metal hammer (Mjöllnir) that was powerful and magical. It could be thrown, and it would then boomerang back to the wielder. Yet, due to Loki's interference, the hammer had one flaw: it's handle was short, making it ungainly to wield.

The dwarves traveled to Asgard to present their costly gifts and claim their fees. Thor was given the hammer and the golden hair for Sif. Odin claimed Draupnir as well as Gungnir. Freyr was awarded with Skidbladnir and Gullinbursti. For his treachery, Loki was given to the dwarves as payment, who sewed his lips shut.

Thor Goes Fishing for Jormungand

The gods were going to host a massive feast with the two ocean giants Aegir and Ran who offered to brew mead for all the gods who would attend. However, this would require a massive kettle to brew the honeyed wine in as the gods were many and had legendary appetites. The only kettle large enough to brew such a massive batch of mead was owned by the giant Hymir who was hardly friendly towards the gods.

Thor, being brave and well-versed in communicating with the giants, offered to go to Hymir to ask for the kettle. When Thor arrived at Hymir's home, the giant slaughtered three bulls to provide meat for them during Thor's visit. However, Thor had a legendary appetite, and he easily devoured two of the three bulls in one meal.

The giant angrily said they would have to go fishing for the next day's food since there wasn't enough meat left over. Thor happily agreed, and Hymir sent him to get bait for the fishing trip. He didn't consider that Thor would slaughter his prized bull with the intention of using the bull's head as bait. Enraged, Hymir wanted to take vengeance against Thor, but he also hoped the young god's strength and courage would help them in their fishing trip.

Boarding a boat, Thor began rowing. They first visited Hymir's regular fishing waters, where the giant easily caught two whales to eat. Thor then pulled up anchor and began to row, but he wasn't rowing back to land. Instead, Thor was rowing them out to deeper water, and Hymir became anxious.

The deep ocean was where the terrifying serpent Jormungand lived!

He begged Thor to turn back to land. However, Thor anchored the boat and cast his line with the bull's head as bait. After some time, a massive pull almost capsized the boat. Thor held onto the fishing rod with all of his prodigious strength, bracing so hard that the boards at the bottom of the boat buckled and began to leak. After a short struggle, the head of the grotesque sea serpent rose above the water, the cruel hook caught in its mouth.

Grinning, Thor reached for his hammer, ready to slay the beast, but Hymir panicked and cut the line to save his boat. Thor had missed out on the opportunity to slay the beast. Angry at the giant, Thor threw him into the waves, then he tossed the two whales over his broad shoulders and waded to shore. Taking both the whales and the giant's cauldron, he returned to Asgard for the feast.

Baldur

Son of Frigg and Odin, Baldur was also reportedly handsome and fiercely brave. He was associated with light and cheerfulness. He was known as the god of love, truth, and light. The only substantial myth concerning him is the story of his death and the attempts to resurrect him. Baldur married the goddess Nanna, and their child was Forseti, who later became the god of justice.

Baldur had long hair and a coarse beard. While he was masculine and handsome, Baldur was not an aggressive god, which made him well-liked by all. Depictions of him often show him as an attractive man who is armed with a spear and a shield, but these are usually not held in his hands as if for combat, but they are rather lying on the ground.

Living in a palace called Breidablik, Baldur and his wife Nanna were popular among the Midguardians. Baldur was known to possess knowledge of runes and herbs, which he used to heal the sick and injured.

Baldur's Death and Attempts at Resurrection

Baldur was considered the fairest of the gods, and such was his pleasant nature that all loved him. When he suddenly began having troubling dreams of his own death, he spoke to his mother Frigg, who was a powerful sorceress and goddess. She instantly turned to

Odin, Baldur's father, and implored him to find out what these dreams meant.

Odin knew a dead seeress who dwelt in the underworld (Helheim), and dressed in a disguise as a wandered, Odin rode upon his eight-legged steed, Sleipnir, down to the depths of Helheim. Reaching the cold and desolate realm of Helheim, Odin was amazed to see a feast had been laid out, as if expecting some important guest. He began questioning the seeress, who happily told him they were awaiting the arrival of a prominent guest who was sure to die soon. She was about to tell Odin how the guest was supposed to die when she looked at Odin and wondered at the panic in his questions. Finally, she only revealed that the guest was Baldur, but she refrained from saying how the godling was going to die.

Crestfallen, Odin returned to Asgard and related all that he had learned to Frigg, who was inconsolable upon the news that her beloved son would die. In desperation, Frigg traveled to all of the realm, begging and securing promises from every living thing that they would not harm her son. Even the rocks and sand gave their consent that they would not harm Baldur. He became invincible.

Such was his new power and safety from harm that the other gods would make a sport out of throwing anything they could lie their hands on at Baldur, watching these bounce harmlessly off him. Nothing could harm Baldur, it seemed.

Of course, Loki wouldn't approve of such a sport, unless he was the maker of it, so he decided to wreak havoc. Donning a disguise, he asked Frigg if she had really gotten all things to give their consent not to harm Baldur. This was truly an amazing feat, and Frigg was happy to admit she had gotten all these consents, but then as a side note, she admitted that she had not acquired consent from the mistletoe, which was so soft and kind it wouldn't harm her son in any case.

Gleefully, Loki left and went to the first mistletoe tree, carving a spear from its trunk. Then he approached Hodr, a god who was blind, and seeming to sympathize with Hodr, who couldn't participate in the other gods' fun by throwing things at Baldur, Loki passed him the spear and suggested he throw the spear at Baldur to also join the fun. Loki helped Hodr aim and then disappeared as the blind god threw the spear.

The spear sailed through the air, cleaving into Baldur, who dropped dead. The gods were in a state of panic and fear. While they were anguished that Baldur had been slain, they were also afraid since this was reportedly one of the first signs of the impending doom of Ragnarok. Frigg was beside herself with grief, but she finally asked if there was a brave enough god there who could journey to Helheim and entreat Hel to release her son that he may be resurrected. There was nothing that Frigg and Odin wouldn't pay in ransom.

Hermod, a lesser son of Odin, stepped forward and swore to do this task. Odin quickly placed Hermod upon his own steed, Sleipnir, and sent him off to the underworld. On the journey to Helheim, Hermod traveled for nine days and nights to reach the river Gjoll, which was guarded by a giantess Modgud. She asked why he would want to enter Helheim when he was still among the living, but Hermod cleverly told her that he had come to negotiate for a relative's release from death. Satisfied, the giantess let him pass into Helheim. Reaching Hel's enclosure, Hermod didn't enter by the gate, but instead, he leapt the wall with Sleipnir and snuck closer to the area where a massive feast was happening.

There, Hermod saw Hel sitting with the cold and pale Baldur next to her. Hermod approached Hel and began to entreat her to release Baldur that he may be resurrected in the world above. However, Hel wasn't interested in letting go of her latest pet.

Finally, in an act of spite, Hel said that if all beings in creation could weep for Baldur, then she would release him. With this news, Hermod rode Sleipnir back to Asgard where he told Frigg what she had to do to secure her son's release.

Frigg easily secured the tears of all living things in creation except for one giantess, Tokk, who responded by saying that she wouldn't cry and Hel could keep what she had. This giantess was, of course, Loki in disguise. And so, Baldur remained in Helheim, never to be resurrected again.

Following the full death of Baldur, the Aesir decided to give him a magnificent funeral. In Viking tradition, they prepared his great ship, Hringhorni, stacking it with kindling as they lay Baldur's body on the craft. As they were preparing to torch the funeral pyre, the gods realized the ship had become stuck in the beach sand. They were unable to heave it into the waters, so they were forced to call on the strength of the giantess Hyrrokkin to push the craft into the ocean.

When Hyrrokkin arrived in Asgard, she rode in on the back of a wolf, and she used two poisonous snakes for reins. One can imagine what a terrifying sight she was. Even her name meant "shriveled by fire." Taking hold of the ship, she gave one terrific shove, launching the ship into the ocean.

While the ship was in the shallows, Baldur's wife, Nanna, had a heart attack and died on the spot. As was tradition, the gods placed her body with Baldur's on the ship as well as leading his horse aboard. The fire was then lit, and Thor blessed the funeral pyre with his hammer.

~~~~~//~~~~~

The royal family of Asgard was quite extensive, with Odin having many sons who are occasionally mentioned in the *Poetic Edda*. While these tales are quite strange and unusual, they do cover themes that humans deal with on a daily basis. Odin's sacrifices to gain treasures and knowledge appealed to the beliefs of the Norse that achievement is only found through self-sacrifice. Frigg's tragic efforts to protect her son indicates a very real human challenge to stave off death.

Thor's myths center around being brave in the face of overwhelming odds, facing your nemesis, and acting with courage. Baldur's story is one of warning: never to take life for granted, as you never know when a spear might slay you (even one cast by a blind god). The other Asgardian gods provided other valuable tales and experiences to learn from and reflect on.

Chapter 5:

Asgardians

Image 13: Steven Erixon on Unsplash. The stories of the Asgardians are recorded on the rune rocks scattered all across the Scandinavian lands, and in these strange writings, we can learn all about Odin, the other gods and goddesses, and the trials they went through.

Tyr

Little is known about Tyr, and like many other gods and goddesses who have faded into the past due to oral traditions not being captured in writing, we may have lost a large chunk of what was known of him. Tyr's weapons were a spear and magical gloves. While history and time has all but forgotten this noble god, we do know he was once revered as one of the prime gods of the Aesir by the Norse tribes.

Remembered still in the naming of Tuesday, Tyr was associated with justice and order. However, he was also revered as a battle god and honored for his bravery and courage in battle. Well established as one of the main war gods, Tyr held his place with Thor and Odin when it came to battles. Early Norsemen would invoke his blessings before entering battle. While Loki accused Tyr of only being able to cause conflict between people, Tyr was more concerned with justice than warmongering.

During Ragnarok, Tyr was destined to battle the hellhound Garm. While it was foretold that he would slay the beast, he would be so severely injured that he would also succumb to his injuries and ultimately die. This is an appropriate conclusion to the tale of the binding of Fenrir, which is said to be the same as the hellhound Garm. In slaying Garm/Fenrir, Tyr could finally take retribution for the loss he suffered when he bound Fenrir.

He ruled in disputes, and his actions contributed in settling conflict between the gods. In the story of the binding of Fenrir, Tyr preserves peace at great personal cost. His psychological instruction is then that it is better to sacrifice than to encourage strife.

The Binding of Fenrir

Loki, being ever the contrary god, had sired three offspring with the giantess Angrboda (meaning: she who bodes anguish). These terrible beasts had posed some trouble to the gods who were unsure of their destiny in the scheme of things. Thus, to maintain some control over them, the gods sent Hel to Helheim, and they confined Jormungand to the sea that surrounded Midgard. However, they especially feared Fenrir, the massive wolf pup. Him they didn't want to let out of their sight, and so, they decided to raise this offspring of Loki where they could keep an eye on it and bind it.

Yet, Fenrir grew more powerful with each passing day, and while the gods tried to come up with a plan on how to bind the beast, the wolf easily broke through any bindings they placed on it.

Wolves, being clever beasts, were not easily deceived, and the beast refused to have any bindings placed on it. Only by pretending they were training the beast to grow stronger could they get it to agree to being bound. And only Tyr who was the most just among them could get close enough to wrap chains and ropes around its limbs. Each time the wolf broke through a new set of chains, the gods cheered and pretended to be in awe so they could convince the wolf to let them put more powerful bindings on it in future.

Meanwhile, the gods grew desperate in their fear of the mighty beast. They sent an envoy to the dwarfs of Svartalfheim, asking the dwarves to use their incredible skill and craftsmanship to make a binding that could finally keep the wolf bound for all eternity. The dwarves came up with an unusual solution: They fashioned a chain out of the soft padding sound of a cat's steps, a woman's beard, the deepest roots of a mountain, a fish's breath, and a bird's spit. By using things that didn't exist, the dwarves made a binding that Fenrir couldn't oppose.

The magical chain was light as a feather, and the dwarves had named it Gleipnir (meaning: open), and it was the only thing in the cosmos that could bind Fenrir if it was tightly fitted.

Now, with all the preceding bindings the gods had tested on Fenrir, the beast had only allowed the bravest and most honorable of the gods, namely Tyr, to come close enough to bind it. However, Fenrir had grown mistrustful of the bindings the gods wanted to tie and chain it down with. So, it demanded that the god who placed the new binding on it needed to place their arm in his great jaws as surety of their pure intentions. None of the gods were willing to risk this except for Tyr who placed his arm in the wolf's jaws while binding it with Gleipnir.

When Fenrir realized this chain was stronger than him and he couldn't break it, he snapped his jaws close, amputating Tyr's arm. So, Tyr secured the deal at the cost of his limb. With Fenrir bound, the gods moved him to a place that was far away and completely isolated. They set a sword between his jaws, forcing the wolf to keep his mouth open so he might never chew through the chains.

Legend has it that the drool that dribbled from the wolf's open mouth became a river known as Ván (meaning: expectation). Fenrir was forced to wait in this miserable state until he was freed during Ragnarok.

Bragi—The Bard God

It's unclear if Bragi was a god named after a real bard, Bragi Boddason, or if the Norsemen were so in awe of Bragi's skills that they believed he was elevated to godhood upon his death. Either way, Bragi was known as the bard god. He was said to entertain the brave dead in Odin's hall with his wonderful tales. Such was his skill that it was rumored he had runes carved upon his tongue.

Bragi was married to the goddess Idun, who symbolized youth and vitality, and even his name was said to have inspired the word for "poetry." His symbols were the harp, lyre, and other traditional bard's instruments. He was especially venerated on long winter nights, around traditional log fires, and in front of fireplaces where stories were told and tales were sung. Traditional throat drumming may have originated in Bragi's traditions. There are few complete stories involving Bragi as the protagonist, but he features prominently in the poem "Lokasenna."

Bragi Confronts Loki

In the "Lokasenna," Loki arrives uninvited to a feast at Odin's hall. He tries to force entry, but Bragi tells him that his kind is not welcome in this hall. However, Bragi is overruled when Odin invites Loki inside. Loki then toasted all the gods and goddesses, except for Bragi, whom he singled out as being unworthy of his toast.

Bragi responded by offering his arm band, a horse, and a fine sword to Loki as appeasement gifts, since he warns Loki not to anger the gods. When Loki tells Bragi off and remarks that Bragi is always impressed by dishonorable gifts, Bragi threatens that if they had been outside, he would have cut Loki's head from his shoulders. At this point, Idun intercedes and calms Bragi, preventing all-out conflict. However, Loki insults her as embracing her brother's slayer, hinting that Bragi may have slain Idun's own brother. Bragi doesn't feature again in this tale.

Idun—The Goddess of Rejuvenation

The goddess Idun's claim to notoriety is her magical fruits (represented as apples), which she gave to the gods, ensuring their immortality. Therefore, Idun was a vital personage to the gods of Asgard. She was married to Bragi, and she always appeared as a beautiful young maiden. The magical apples (although this is probably an error in the recorded history as the Norse didn't know apples until much later in history) were kept in a box made from ash wood. Her importance is emphasized in the story of her kidnapping.

The Kidnapping of Idun

Idun provided magical fruits to the gods. These fruits or nuts were enriched with immortality. The gods had never before had to face such a dilemma. What would they do if the gods lost their immortality?

In the tale, three gods (Odin, Loki, and Hoenir) were traveling far from Asgard into the desolate lands. Feeling really hungry, the gods slaughtered a herd of oxen they came upon. However, once they had built a fire, the meat would not roast on these flames and they couldn't cook their meal.

"This is my doing, gods of Asgard," a voice said from above them. It was a giant eagle, sitting in the tree. "With my magical powers, I have frozen your flames. If you will give me my share of the meat, then I will let you cook the rest of the oxen."

Unable to deny their hunger, they agreed with the eagle, who ate the very best sections of meat from the ox, leaving only the stringy bits for the gods to eat. The gods were enraged, but what else could they do?

Loki was unhappy with this bargain, and he decided to kill the eagle with his club as it was busy devouring the meat. However, much to Loki's surprise, the eagle spun, grabbed the club and launched into the sky with the surprised Loki still clinging on to the weapon. The eagle flew high into the air with Loki still hanging there.

Begging for the eagle to let him down, Loki's pleas fell on deaf ears, and the eagle (which was actually the giant Thjazi in disguise) flew back to his mountain nest. In this eagle's nest, the eagle struck a deal with Loki. If Loki could give Idun and her immortal fruits to the eagle/giant, then it would release him.

Loki rejoined the other gods and returned to Asgard. Once there, Loki tricked Idun to follow him as he had found fruits more magical than her very own. Idun followed Loki to a forest that surrounded Asgard where Thjazi swooped in as a giant eagle, grabbed Idun and her magic fruits, and sped off.

With immortality removed from Asgard, the other gods and goddesses began to shrivel and grow old. The gods, realizing they would grow old and die, were desperate to have Idun and her fruits returned. They were still unaware of her kidnapping or of Loki's involvement. However, they quickly put the pieces of the puzzle together and found out that she'd last been in Loki's company in the great forest.

The gods seized Loki, threatening him terribly until he spilled the beans and admitted to being a part of her kidnapping. The gods demanded that Idun be returned, but Thjazi had taken her to his home, the mountain stronghold of Thrymheim.

Freya gave her hawk feathers to Loki, allowing him to turn into a hawk that he might fly to the mountain stronghold on Jotunheim and rescue Idun and her fruit. Once Loki arrived, he was thrilled to find the fortress abandoned, except for Idun and her fruits. He quickly changed the goddess into a nut so he might easily carry her, and gripping the nut in his talons, he flew as fast as he could back to Asgard, knowing the giant would be in hot pursuit as soon as he found out his prize had been stolen away.

Loki was drawing near to Asgard when the giant eagle started to gain on him. The gods had been watching the skies in desperation as they waited for Idun's return, so they saw the great race happening overhead. They built a large bonfire near Asgard's wall. As Loki flew over with the eagle close behind, the gods lit the fire at that moment, and it exploded, roasting the eagle in the sky.

Idun was safely returned, and that is where the story ends, though we can imagine there were some serious repercussions for Loki for having betrayed Idun to the eagle in the first place.

Image 14: Russo self-designed image. The great horn of Heimdall, Gjallarhorn, was said to herald the start of Ragnarok.

Heimdall

The guardian of the Bifröst, Heimdall is the defender and watchman of Asgard. His home, Himinbjörg (meaning: sky cliffs) is perched high above the Bifröst, and it gives Heimdall a bird's eye view of any approaching enemies. Heimdall has some excellent abilities, including that he sleeps less than a bird, can see for hundreds of miles with the clarity of an eagle, and he can hear grass grow and even wool growing on a sheep's back. Truly, he is equipped to be an ever-present watchman who sees all that happens in and around Asgard.

When the great horn of Heimdall, the Gjallarhorn, sounds an alarm, it will signal the start of Ragnarok and the approach of the giants coming to slay the gods in Asgard. It is fated that during this conflict, Heimdall and Loki would slay each other as the world went up in flames around them.

Heimdall is also born of Odin, and in a magical twist, he has nine mothers called the Nine Undines. Their names are representative of the power of the ocean.

First, there was Duva (meaning: hidden one) and also Kolga (meaning: cold one), who reminds one of the ocean depths. Then came Blodughadda who had red hair and was truly bloodthirsty. She was named after the red tide when the very seafoam would turn red. Fourth was Bara (meaning: foam fleck), which referred to the moment a wave hit the shore. There was also Bylgja (meaning: billow), which might refer to the wind over the sea in the ships sails or the breaching of whales when they blow. Hrǫnn (meaning: wave welling) and her twin sister Hefring (meaning: wave that rises) were also known for their blood-thirsty appetites. Unn was named for frothing waves, while the youngest of the sisters, Himinglava was the transparency of waves. These were the nine sisters who were said to have covered for each other when Odin slept with one of them, conceiving Heimdall. However, there is also a rumor that Odin had slept with all nine of these ferocious maidens (quite the feat) and one of them fell pregnant with Heimdall.

The number nine features quite strongly in Norse mythology. While Heimdall is involved in many stories, he is rarely the central figure. However, he is known as the father of all humans, not to be confused with the Allfather as Odin was known. Heimdall was said to have visited three married couples in the beginning when Midgard was made. He stayed with a poor family, then a farmer and his wife, and lastly, a wealthy lady and lord. Nine months after his visit, all three couples were blessed with a child each.

These children were respectively Thrall who was strong but ugly and became the ancestor of the serfs or slaves; next, Karl was skilled with the land, and he became the ancestor of all farmers; and, lastly was Jarl, who was the first of the noble classes.

Heimdall appears in the story of the building of the wall of Asgard, and he also features in the story of Ragnarok. We'll be looking more closely at those in the following chapters.

~~~~~//~~~~~

Chapter 3 and Chapter 4 has given us an idea of what the Asgardian gods were like, the tales they were involved in, and the adventures they enjoyed. Now it's time to look at the Vanir gods in more detail. The conflict and unity between these two god tribes are not only a major axis in Norse mythology but also representative of the conflict the warring tribes of the Viking era faced.

Chapter 6:

The Vanir

Image 14: Russo self-designed image. The Vanir were gods of nature, wealth, abundance, fertility, and magic. They were the very opposite of the Asgardians who were brawnier, relying on their brute strength as opposed to magic.

Njord—The God of Seas and Wealth

One of the most prominent Vanir gods, Njord was sent as hostage to the Aesir after the Aesir-Vanir war in a prisoner exchange. The early Vikings believed that Njord was the god of the sea. They believed he could control the wind and the waves, and he was said to be immeasurably rich. Hence, the expression "to be as rich as Njord."

Njord's two children Freyr and Freya also accompanied him to Asgard where they were well received. While these two gods were supposedly begotten by Njord with his own sister, he later wedded a giantess named Skadi. This union was doomed though as Skadi loved the ice and snow of winter, while Njord loved the milder climates of the ocean.

Fate decreed that Njord would be one of the few Norse gods to survive Ragnarok.

The Marriage of Skadi and Njord

This tale came about as Idun was returned with her magical fruits to Asgard following her kidnapping. The gods, having suffered greatly the effects of old age while she had been gone, were reveling in the sun and warm glow of their restored youth.

Skadi was meanwhile waiting for the return of her father, Thjazi; however, she knew deep inside that her father had been murdered. Finally, after a night and a day, Skadi gathered up her spear and her hide-covered shield. She took her father's sword with special runes engraved on the blade and set off to Asgard, ready to seek vengeance.

Now, the gods were in a light spirit after regaining their immortality, so they had no wish for further bloodshed against the giantess as she neared Asgard. Heimdall sounded the alarm with his great horn, and the gods gathered to face the angry giantess. At first, they offered her money in exchange for the loss of her father, but she retorted that she had no need of more wealth as her father had been wealthy beyond comparison.

Finally, Odin asked what would satisfy her sorrow and her need for revenge. The giantess replied that she would choose a husband from among the gods (keeping her eyes on the beautiful Baldur) and she would laugh again. The giantess believed these two tasks would be beyond the Asgardians and she could then have her revenge.

So, Odin agreed upon the condition that Skadi choose a husband by only seeing his feet and legs. She agreed, and the gods blindfolded her so she could only see a small section above the ground, where the male gods lined up so she could view their legs. Believing that only Baldur could have the most shapely legs, and she chose quickly. Believing that everything was perfect on a god as handsome as Baldur, she chose the most attractive legs she could see. However, when she saw who the legs belonged to, she was shocked. The husband she had chosen was none other than Njord, the sea god!

Skadi began to complain, saying she'd been tricked, but Njord cautioned her to think carefully as her words were the start of their marriage. Njord further teased her that her choice could have been Loki, so she ought to count herself lucky. Still confident she would outwit the gods, Skadi announced she had not laughed since her father's death and she was unlikely to laugh now. So, Odin called upon Loki, having full confidence in the trickster's ability to make the giantess laugh.

Loki was somewhat bashful, which is contrary to his nature, but he had been the reason her father had kidnapped Idun and he had also been the reason Thjazi had been killed as he flew over Asgard's walls. Hoping the giantess would never learn the truth, Loki set out to make her laugh—no mean feat considering her frozen countenance.

So, taking a leather thong from his pocket, Loki told Skadi he had been to market and with his arms laden with food and parcels, he had no hand left to hold his goat's leash. In desperation, Loki had apparently tied the goat to a sensitive part of his body, making the beast follow him home.

"What 'sensitive part?'" Skadi asked, a bemused expression on her face.

"Well, lady, I had no option but to tie the beast to my … uhm … testicle," Loki said and began to demonstrate by tying the leather thong to his testicle on one end and to the goat's beard on the other. When the goat pulled back, Loki squealed in pain, and when Loki pulled back, the goat bleated in agony. It was a tug of war! Finally, in pain, Loki stumbled backward and fell in the giantess's lap, and unable to stop herself, she chuckled softly.

Thus, having secured the giantess's laughter, she and Njord were wedded. Odin, in an act of wisdom, further appeased the giantess's sorrow by producing her father's eyes, which he cast into the night sky where they became stars, looking down on her always.

Njord had planned they should live in his home by the seas of Asgard, but Skadi wanted no such thing. So, they compromised, and decided to live nine days and nights in Thrymheim, high in the mountains of Jotunheim, where there was only ice and snow and wolves howling at the moon. Njord was most unhappy, hating everything about Skadi's home.

They then traveled to his home on the shores of Asgard's seas, and stayed nine days and nights in Noatun, where the seas whispered and the gulls cried every morning and night. Skadi was most unhappy there, and realizing they could never live together, they decided to live separately. Njord remained in Noatun, and Skadi returned to Thrymheim.

Freyr—The God of Fertility and Weather, Peace, and Prosperity

Freyr, like his father Njord, was sent as hostage to Asgard following the Aesir-Vanir war. He was known as the god of fertility, prosperity, and abundance. He was, therefore, one of the most loved gods to Norse peoples as he blessed marriages with children, and he was represented with an enormous erect phallus. His totemic animal was the golden boar Gullinborsti. Freyr chose to live among the elves on Alfheim where he was lord of the elves. Even his name Freyr meant "lord" in old Norse.

While Freyr was a skilled and experienced fighter, he was popular with the farmer and serf class of Norsemen because he could secure crops and children for his followers. This meant they could feed themselves and have families, which, in an odd way, made Freyr the protector of the simple man (and woman) too. Most Aesir gods were venerated for their war-like abilities, but Freyr was worshipped for his ability to bring peace and prosperity, revealing the duality of Norse culture.

Freyr was known for his magical sword, which could fight on its own, and he also had the golden boar the dwarves had made. In addition to this, he also had a superior horse called Blodughofi, which means "blood hoof." But most spectacular among his treasures was surely the magical ship Skidbladnir, which was the fastest vessel on the oceans, and it could fold into his pocket. It was also rumored to be unsinkable and always steered true.

According to legend, Freyr traveled by sea with this magical ship, which was made by the dwarves from thin slivers of wood. On land, when Freyr wasn't astride his magnificent warhorse, he traveled in a chariot drawn by wild boars. As Freyr was the god of love, lust, and fertility, his appeal to both goddesses and giantesses was well noted.

Freyr and Gerdr

In Odin's hall, there was a special seat called Hliðskjálf, which allowed anyone who sat upon it a view into all nine worlds. Freyr had the opportunity to sit on this seat, and gazing throughout the realms, he saw a woman, a giantess, who was so fair as to steal his heart.

Freyr was so overcome with grief at the thought of never having this woman, he fell into a deep depression, wasting away. Concerned, his father, Njord, sent his servant Skirnir to check on Freyr and find out what ailed him. Freyr confessed his longing for the giantess Gerdr, and that if he could not have her, life was not worth living.

Skirnir said he would go woo the giantess for Freyr, but Freyr had to give "the sword of Freyr," his magical sword that could fight on its own, to Skirnir to take with. Freyr agreed without any second thoughts, and the servant set off to woo the giantess.

This had seemed a small price to Freyr in exchange for Gerdr's consent to marry him, but the cost would be more than he could imagine, as this exchange meant he would have to face the giant Surt without his magical sword during Ragnarok. Ultimately, it would lead to his death.

Freya—The Goddess of Fate and Destiny

Sister to Freyr and daughter to Njord, Frey was the goddess of virility, blessings, and love. She was a milder version of the other gods, and her talent was more in the realms of magic than that of physical combat. While she was said to be gentle and mostly achieved her goals with bargaining and by using sex as a tactic, she was also known to be the most fearsome killer on the battlefield, claiming more than half the dead during conflict.

Despite her darker side in conflict, Freya's name meant "lady."

Having mastered the art of the seidr, Freya could change the future and influence the past. It is said that she taught this skill, which was primarily a woman's magic, to Odin.

With Freya and Frigg sometimes being the same goddess and being able to predict the future, she gave the fated prediction regarding Ragnarok and the death of the gods when the giants attacked. She also predicted the falling of Asgard and the burning of Odin's hall.

Friday is likely named after her, and the lustful nature of this goddess is captured in the revelry that usually accompanies Fridays when people celebrate the end of the work week.

While Odin welcomed half of the slain dead to his hall of Valhalla, Freya ruled the other half in her palace at Sessrúmnir (meaning: seat room), which was located in the Fólkvangr (meaning: field of the host).

Freya married an obscure god named Odr, which is thought to have been Odin. This has caused some confusion about whether Freya and Frigg were actually the same goddess. With Odr, she had two children, Gersemi and Hnoss. Some narratives portrayed Freya as a goddess of loose morals who was willing to turn tricks for any fancy trinket that she desired. If Freya and Frigg were indeed the same goddess, then it explains why Odin was so obsessed with Freya.

Odin's obsessions are manifested in the story of Freya and the golden torc. It once again shows Loki's ever-present annoyance and manipulations that interfered with the affairs of the gods.

Freya didn't have any special weapons, but she did possess many magical objects that she used to reach her own goals. She owned a cloak with falcon feathers, which she used to fly with or transform into a falcon. It is from here that she plucked a few feathers to transform Loki into a falcon so that he may rescue Idun from the giant when she had been kidnapped. She also had a torc, Brísingamen (meaning: gleaming torc), which she was quite obsessed with. She allegedly purchased this torc from the four dwarves who gave it to her upon her agreeing to have sex with each of them. Freya also had a golden chariot drawn by two blue cats.

Freya and the Golden Torc

Freya loved all things beautiful. When she saw the golden necklace being made by four dwarves in a darkened cave, she instantly wanted it. The dwarves were born opportunists, and they demanded that Freya sleep with each of them in turn. Loki, always lurking in the shadows, happened to pass near the cave, and he witnessed Freya copulating with the dwarves in exchange for the necklace.

Aiming to sow discord among the Aesir gods, Loki revealed this to Odin, who was furious. He instructed Loki to retrieve the necklace that Freya loved so much and bring it to him.

Loki turned into a flea and managed to get into the goddess's sealed tower that night. Freya lay sleeping on her bed, the golden necklace clasped around her neck. Such was the position of her head that Loki was unable to retrieve the necklace. So, he bit her on the cheek, making her turn over in her sleep. Now Loki could slip the necklace off, and taking it, he quickly scurried off to the waiting Odin.

When Freya awoke, she was distraught to discover her beloved necklace was gone. Believing there to be a thief on Asgard, Freya went to Odin to complain. However, Odin coldly revealed that he had the necklace and also knew how she had come by it. Freya begged forgiveness. However, Odin said he would only give back her necklace if she performed a certain task for him. She had to cause two kings (who each ruled over 20 kings) to go to war with each other. This was to be an endless war though, and Freya did this to regain her treasure. These kings fought for years, and they only knew peace when Olaf Tryggvason, the Christian King of Norway, gained power.

Tales such as this one did not do much to build the goddess's reputation, and while it may have been a smear campaign by early Christians, it did discredit Freya by portraying her as a whore.

Freya and the Building of the Wall of Asgard

Freya had been greatly desired by the giants, and when a giant approached Asgard, offering to rebuild their wall within a short time and to impenetrable strength in exchange for marriage to Freya, it seemed like a good deal to the other gods. They agreed upon the condition that the giant, whose name is never mentioned, complete the wall within one year.

Within a matter of months, the gods noticed that the giant did indeed seem capable of building the wall in a year, since his stallion, Svadilfari, was strong and powerful and managed to do most of the work for the giant by moving stones on its broad back. The gods were fearing they might have to sacrifice Freya in exchange for the wall if the giant could uphold his end of the deal.

However, sly Loki came up with a plan. He transformed himself into a beautiful mare and so tempted the stallion that he was no longer capable of working with the giant, and the work fell behind schedule. The giant, realizing he had been tricked and wouldn't be able to finish the wall on time, became enraged and he grew aggressive. In fear, the gods called on Thor to come save them from the ferocious giant. Thor arrived, and without a second thought, he drew his mighty hammer and smote the giant, killing him instantly.

So, Asgard gained an impressive wall and Freya was safe from having to wed the giant. In a strange twist, Loki who had been entertaining the giant's stallion had been impregnated and foaled, giving birth to a colt named Sleipnir, which he gifted to Odin. This magnificent horse had eight legs and was the fastest and most powerful horse ever known.

In another twisted story, Freya was again almost pawned off as a bride to a giant when Thor's hammer disappeared.

The Disappearance of Thor's Hammer and Freya's Wedding

Thor awoke one morning to find that Mjöllnir, his powerful hammer, was missing! He was so upset that his hair stood on end and his beard bristled. As one can imagine, he must have been quite a terrifying image. When he finally did calm down somewhat, Thor went to the other gods, asking their help to find Mjöllnir.

The other gods were all upset as well. With Thor's powerful hammer missing, Asgard was vulnerable to attack! They all set out to find Mjöllnir as quickly as possible, and even Loki borrowed Freya's falcon cloak to go find the hammer.

With these swift wings to assist him, Loki flew to Jotunheim. He soon discovered that the giant Thrym (meaning: noisy) had indeed taken Thor's hammer. Thrym had hidden the hammer more than eight miles below the earth, and he was only willing to return it on one condition: that Freya marries him.

Now, the gods were not at all interested in this union, and serious debate raged in Asgard as the gods tried to come up with a solution. While they wouldn't willingly lose Freya to a giant in marriage, they also couldn't afford to lose Thor's hammer, which was their primary weapon for Ragnarok.

Heimdall was known for his wisdom and insight, and he came up with a solution. The gods would send Thor disguised as Freya to "marry" the giant, and once the giant produced Mjöllnir, Thor could then grab his hammer and strike at the giant. As you can imagine, Thor was less than pleased with this plan as it meant he would have to dress like a woman! He feared that all of Asgard would jest with him for all of eternity (since the gods were immortal, they would literally never forget), and he believed he couldn't live with the shame.

However, Loki cleverly pointed out that without Mjöllnir, Asgard would be overrun by giants when Ragnarok came, which would mean even more shame for Thor. Grudgingly, Thor agreed to the plan and allowed the gods to dress him up in a suitable wedding dress with a thick veil to hide his masculinity. Loki agreed to also dress in disguise as "Freya's" maid-servant, thus hiding their real intent. Thus, Loki and the disguised Thor traveled to Jotunheim for the wedding.

Thor was well-known for his incredible appetite, and at the wedding feast, he almost gave up the clever plot when he ate a huge spread of food, including one ox, eight salmon, all the pastries and tarts that the women were supposed to eat, and drank enough mead to drown a sailor.

Thrym began to suspect that something was amiss with his new bride, and he remarked heavily, "Never in all my many long years have I seen a woman eat and drink as you, Lady Freya."

Knowing that Thor couldn't disguise his heavy timbered voice, Loki quickly interceded, and he replied in a high-pitched voice, "The lady Freya has been starving herself for days with want for seeing you, my Lord!"

Now, Thrym accepted this response as he was already quite full with mead too, and he suddenly couldn't resist the urge to kiss his bride, so he pulled back Thor's upper veil, but when he saw Thor's burning eyes, he was stunned.

Blushing at the dark look in his bride's eyes, Thrym remarked that he had never before seen such a look of passion in a maiden's eyes, to which Loki again replied in his feminine tone of voice, "The Lady Freya has been so excited at the thought of her wedding night that she hasn't been able to sleep for days, Lord Thrym."

Then followed the ceremony, and as was tradition, Mjöllnir was brought forth to sanctify the union between Thrym and "Freya." But as soon as the hammer was placed in Thor's lap, he grabbed it and smote the giant and the rest of the wedding guests in a bloody rage. Happy to have his beloved hammer back in his control, Thor traveled back to Asgard where he jauntily changed back into his own clothes.

Image 15: Enrique Meseguer from Pixabay. War was a common occurrence of the gods. They regularly engaged in battles, waged conflicts, and went off to slay creatures. This may have been a mimicry of the tribes of Scandinavia that often raided, looted, and made war on neighboring tribes. The war of the Aesir-Vanir was one such conflict between the gods.

The Aesir-Vanir War

While the focus of Norse Mythology seems to always be on the end days of Ragnarok, we should not neglect the tale of the Aesir-Vanir War, when the Aesir and the Vanir battled without cease. While the two godly races were later unified, this was a time of great bloodshed and sorrow. However, only through the prisoner exchange did the Asgardian gods, like Odin and even some of the other gods, gain their magical powers.

The Aesir hailed from Asgard, and they were renowned for their physical prowess in battle, while the Vanir were from Vanaheim, and they were known for their magical ways. Freya, who was a sorceress without par, wandered the worlds of Yggdrasil, and using a disguise, she traveled while dispensing her magical skills. The Asgardians knew her only as Heiðr (meaning: bright). It is unclear if things would have turned out differently if the Asgardians had known that Heiðr was secretly Freya, but they became obsessed with her skills.

Chasing after desires and ideals that were against their own laws and warrior codes, the Aesir soon realized they were changing as a people due to their new obsession with magic. So, they decided to blame Freya, and they tried to murder her. Three times they tried to burn her as a witch, but each time she simply protected herself with her magic and walked from the ashes like a phoenix is reborn from its own funeral pyre.

The violent acts of the Aesir against Freya, who was an important figure to the Vanir, soon stirred up feelings of hatred between the two races as they grew to despise each other. It wasn't long before their hostilities blew into open war.

Both sides fought using their respective means. The Aesir fought with terrifying weapons such as Thor's hammer, Odin's spear, and Heimdall's sword. The Vanir used their magic in terrible ways. Both sides suffered terrible losses, and the war raged on for years.

Finally, both sides grew weary of fighting and quarreling, and a truce was called. As was the tradition, the two sides agreed to pay restitution to each other, and the truce was sealed with an exchange of hostages.

As has already been mentioned, the Vanir sent Njord and his two children, Freya and Freyr, to live among the Asgardians, while the Aesir sent Mimir and Hoenir to live on Vanir. One could imagine Freya may not have been happy with living in Asgard after she had been burned three times before by the Asgardians. Likewise, the unfortunate slaying of Mimir caused the Asgardians to feel a surge in hostilities, although the peace held between the two races of gods.

The tale ends with the gods gathering and making the magic mead by all chewing berries and spitting it in a barrel. From this mead, Kvasir, the wisest human, was born.

The Vanir were opposing forces to the Aesir, yet they could set their conflicts aside, even forgiving terrible atrocities committed on both sides, eventually fighting side by side in Ragnarok. While there was great nobility of spirit among the gods, they could be cruel and fickle at other times as we will see in the tale of Loki's binding.

Chapter 7:

Deadly Offspring

Image 16: Russo self-designed image. Loki, being the offspring of two giants, had his own troublesome children that he added to the world of the Norse gods. These would be intricately involved in the final conflict of Ragnarok.

Loki—The Trickster God

The trickster was one of the four main Norse deities, and together with Odin, Freya, and Thor, Loki was the best known and most involved in Norse mythology. Loki was the absolute chameleon, shapeshifting, re-aligning, betraying, and defending the worlds and gods of Yggdrasil. There was incredible duality to Loki's persona, and where he might help Thor one day, he would betray Sif the next. With Loki, what you saw was never what you got. When you try to class Loki as being a good or an evil god, you will fall short as he is neither. Loki is simply an agent of chaos, and he casually upturned the views of others.

His father was the giant Farbauti, and his mother was the giantess Laufey (though there is some uncertainty of her ancestry).

Even the meaning of Loki's name is ambiguous, and it could mean either "fire" or "knot" or even "spider" based on interpretation and usage. Unlike the other gods who had their own accoutrements, Loki only had his wits and shapeshifting powers. Loki had assumed various forms from fish and fleas to birds, and even the old giantess who refused to weep for Baldur. His symbolic animal was a snake.

Loki married the goddess Sigyn, which again was strange, as he is not a half Asgardian like some of the other gods and goddesses. His parentage was fully giant, which makes it strange that he resided in Asgard and was considered an Aesir god. Loki was even able to give birth to another offspring of his own: the eight-legged stallion Sleipnir that he gifted to Odin. There is certainly no more interesting deity than Loki in Norse mythology.

While Thor was powerful, Odin was wise, and Freya possessed magical skills, Loki had intrigues that made him very much a shadowy figure who recklessly influenced the fates of the Aesir, Vanir, and creatures of the Nine Realms alike. It is because of Loki that the end of the world, Ragnarok, takes place.

We may at times feel sorry for Loki, yet his often deceptive and misleading actions are what lands him his fate and the ultimate decision to see Asgard burn.

Loki's Imprisonment

One of the most unpleasant tales is Loki's part in Baldur's death and what happened after. Loki had orchestrated Baldur's death, tricking the blind Hodr into casting a spear made of mistletoe, which was the only living thing that had not given its promise to never harm Baldur. To make matters worse, when Hel agreed to let Baldur be resurrected upon condition that all living things shed tears for him, Loki transformed into the shape of an old giantess, Thökk, and he refused to weep for Baldur. His dismissive attitude towards Baldur is shown in his words: "Let Hel keep what she has then!"

When the gods learned of Loki's involvement, they were beyond enraged, and Odin, having loved his son Baldur dearly, was the most angered. Odin conceived a child, Vali, with the giantess Rindr. Váli grew to manhood in a day and slew Hodr. For Loki, Odin had something far worse in mind.

Loki had realized his taunts and interference in the gods' affairs had made him fall from favor, and following Baldur's death and the gods' inability to resurrect Baldur, Loki fled. Building a house atop a tall mountain, Loki watched day and night for approaching gods who came to claim vengeance for his slaying of Baldur. It is said that he changed into a salmon during the day and hid in a waterfall where nobody could see him. But there was no way to avoid the all-seeing eyes of Odin.

Image 17: Russo self-designed image. Odin sat in his chair Hliðskjálf from where he could see all of Yggdrasil's Nine Realms, and he soon spotted Loki's hiding place.

On one fateful night, Loki was sitting by his fire, mending the net he used to catch fish for food. He saw the gods approaching, and casting his net into the fire, he ran to the river where he transformed into the salmon once more to hide away.

Arriving at Loki's house, the gods saw the net smoldering on the fire, and they quickly decided that Loki must have changed into what he had been catching. They walked to the river, made nets of their own, and surrounded the rocky pool where Loki hid.

Casting their nets in, Loki barely managed to wiggle past their attempts to catch him, but they drew closer and closer, and Loki became desperate to escape.

In one final desperate move, Loki jumped from the water in his fish form and tried to leap into the river leading to the ocean, but mighty Thor had never been slow. In one sweeping gesture, he grabbed the salmon by its tail and held on tightly. The Norse believed this was why salmon have a strangely thin tail fin even today.

What followed was a particularly brutal punishment, which one can only surmise must have angered Loki so that he fought on the side of the giants in Ragnarok, which soon followed.

The gods forced Loki to transform back into his normal form and then they dragged him back to a cave high in the mountain. Here, they brought his two sons with Sigyn to him. The boys, Vali and Narfi, were still young, but the gods transformed Vali into a wolf, who promptly slayed his brother and began eating him while Loki watched. The wolf spilled his brother's entrails all over the cave floor, which then hardened into chains of steel. Taking these, the gods bound Loki to the cave wall.

With Loki bound, the gods then took a venomous snake, which they tied above Loki's head. The snake dripped venom, which burned Loki. To save Loki some pain and suffering, his dutiful wife Sigyn brought a bowl to catch the venom in so it might not drip on his face. The bowl would fill up though, and Sigyn had to go empty it beyond the cave, leaving the drops of venom to drip from the snake onto Loki's face until she returned with the bowl once more.

Each time the venom dripped on Loki's face, it burned him like acid, and Loki writhed in agony. Such was his torment that Loki would convulse with a tremendous force, causing earthquakes to form in Midgard. One can only suspect that Loki must have languished in this agony for years even while he remained chained by his son's entrails. There could not be a grizzlier fate. Eventually Loki would break free, and he would fight against the gods during Ragnarok.

Hel—The Ruler of Helheim and the Realm of the Dead

Hel was the daughter of Loki and the giantess Angrboda, and her name hints at her dark persona as the meaning of Hel is "hidden." She is described as having a face that is half healthy and fleshy colored, and then rotten and skeletal on the other side.

Like the underworld or Helheim (hidden realm) that she governs, Hel is not a friendly person. She is 100% giant, which leaves no doubt where her allegiances lie during Ragnarok. With a giant wolf and a monstrous sea serpent as siblings, this makes for a rather strange and fiendish family.

As we would imagine the ruler of the underworld to be, Hel is not a charitable or kind person. She is rather obsessed with her own goals and her dark purposes of gathering up a host of the dead to fight in the final days of Ragnarok.

Helheim is populated by all people who died of sickness or disease or old age. Only warriors who die in battle can progress up Yggdrasil to reach Valhalla. The rest go down to Helheim. The journey to Helheim is not one that is pleasant or easy. To reach the hall of Hel, one has to travel for nine days and nights through a desolate landscape where the path is known to cut feet to shreds.

Then you need to cross the dangerous river Gjoll with a glass bridge suspended by strings of hair. Falling into the river is best avoided as there are knives floating in the tumultuous waters. The bridge is also guarded by a terrifying giantess, Modgud, whose name doesn't inspire friendly chatter. Her name "furious battle" clearly announces what will happen to those who dare enter without permission or purpose.

The palace in Helheim is surrounded by a tall wall, which has a single gate to allow the dead to enter. Hel rules in the halls of her kingdom as queen of the dead. True to form, all the objects in her hall have misfortunate names. The large table is called hunger, while the knives and forks are called starvation. Her bedroom is equally depressing, and her bed is known as sick-bed while the surrounding curtains are called misfortune.

Image 18: Kristijan Arsov on Unsplash. Warriors who died of old age went to Helheim, while those who died with their sword in their hand went to Valhalla. Needless to say, this fueled the bloodthirsty temperament of the early Viking raiders.

When Hel went collecting the dead on earth (Midgard), she used a rake to choose who she would take to Helheim, but when there was an outbreak of pestilence, she used a broom, simply sweeping the dead into her kingdom.

While the Christian concept of hell is not pleasant, involving torture by terrifying demons, the Norse idea of Helheim wasn't all that bad. When Baldur arrived in Helheim, he was welcomed with a feast of freshly cooked foods, and even Hel herself sat him next to her in her hall.

Hel's Role in Baldur's Remaining Unresurrected

While the story about Baldur's death is more about Loki, we do see some aspect of Hel's character in it too. When Hermod rode into Helheim to ask for Baldur's resurrection, Hel showed little concern for the worlds beyond her own realm. She seemed to have utter disregard for what Baldur's death meant for the end of days. The deal she offered, that every living being in the cosmos must weep for Baldur, was hardly a fair one, especially since her own father was a being in that cosmos, and Loki had been the one who orchestrated Baldur's death.

Fenrir

The giant wolf who would slay Odin at Ragnarok, Fenrir (meaning: dweller in the marshes) was a son of Loki. His sister was Hel, and his other sibling (whose gender isn't really revealed) is Jormungand, the sea serpent. Fenrir is always shown as a slavering wolf who is about to tear up some god (usually Odin).

When the wolf was born, they realized the pup was a terrible force, but they couldn't bring themselves to kill him. So, to try and maintain some control over the beast, the gods took him from his mother, and they raised him themselves. The idea was to stop the wolf from becoming too wild and doing serious damage in the Nine Realms.

However, they were ill prepared for how swiftly the wolf grew. They were soon terrified of him. The only god who was unafraid was Tyr, who could approach the wolf and feed him. Soon, the gods noted the strength and agility that Fenrir possessed, and they realized they would have to chain him up if they wanted to maintain control over him.

So, they had ropes and strong chains made, and while they stood there, pretending the bindings were to make Fenrir stronger, they had Tyr fit these restrictive devices to the wolf. However, twice they tried and twice they failed as the wolf easily broke free from the bindings. The wolf was becoming suspicious as he couldn't understand why the gods would want to tie him down. To fool him, the gods cheered and applauded him for being so strong, saying they only wanted to test him and see just how strong he could be.

Consulting with the dwarves of Svartalfheim, the gods begged the smiths to make a stronger chain or rope, anything they could bind the beast with. The dwarves designed a magical chain that was made from the sound of a cat's footsteps, a woman's beard, a mountain's roots, a bird's spit, and a fish's breath ... all of which were things that didn't technically exist. The reasoning was that since the chain would then not exist within the normal laws of the universe, there would be nothing for Fenrir to fight against, and he would be bound.

When the gods brought the thin little chain to Fenrir, once again saying they wanted to test his strength, the wolf didn't believe them and he became aggressive. The wolf refused to be tied with this little chain, unless one of the gods were to vouch for their honor by putting his arm inside the wolf's mouth. Of course, none of the gods wanted to accept this deal as it would mean the loss of a limb when the wolf discovered he had been tricked.

Brave Tyr, god of truth and justice, stepped forward, laying his arm in the wolf's jaws. As the chain was secured, Fenrir discovered he couldn't break free and in fear and rage, his jaws snapped shut, severing Tyr's arm and swallowing it whole.

Fenrir was sent off to a desolate place where he was chained and bound with a sword to keep his jaws open so he couldn't chew through the chains. There he waited until Ragnarok.

Jormungand

The beast was known as the Midgard serpent, and it was the offspring of the dalliance between Loki and the giantess Angrboda. Jormungand was the beast whose body encircled all of Midgard, which was only protected by the wall the gods had created from Ymir's eyebrows. Thor is the nemesis of the serpent, and it is his archenemy.

While we know of the story where Thor almost slew the serpent when he and the giant Hymir went fishing, their enmity continued, but they would only face off against each other during Ragnarok.

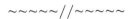

The gods, the magical creatures, and the strange stories of the Norse all culminate in the end times when

Heimdall's horn would blow, signaling the start of Ragnarok. And the horn is finally blowing ...

Chapter 8:

The End Times

Brothers will fight and kill each other,

sisters' children will defile kinship.

It is harsh in the world, whoredom rife

—an axe age, a sword age—shields are riven—

*a wind age, a wolf age—before the world goes
headlong.*

No man will have mercy on another

the Völva, Ursula Dronke translation

Prophecy is rarely pleasant, but there is a certain peace that comes from knowing your end before it begins. This is what accepting your fate is about, and it is a concept central to Viking life and Norse mythology.

The end time prophecy of Ragnarok is the Norse version of the Christian Apocalypse. It is how the world will end in fire. With the prophecies of the witches and seers (such as the Völva), the gods were forewarned of their fate, and while they prepared to meet each other on the battlefield of the end times, they also accepted they would likely not survive the war.

As with all end time stories, there were signs to look for, starting with the death of Beldur. From that point on, a series of cataclysmic events were happening that seemed to defeat all attempts to stop the inevitable. However, like the Vikings, the Norse gods were motivated by proving valor on the battlefield, and for them, death wasn't permanent or even punishment, so they prepared for their fate with remarkable fortitude.

The story of Ragnarok is oddly appealing to people of all cultures as it has themes that we can all relate to: brothers turning against brothers, fighting against impossible odds, courage, honorable death, and rebirth.

Image 20: Russo self-designed image. The final showdown between Thor and Jormungand was just one

of the many battles that happened during the final conflict.

Ragnarok

The series of apocalyptic events that led up to Ragnarok were all in line with the predictions of a nameless fortune teller. For the Vikings, it meant the actual ending of their world, as they believed the gods walked among them. For the Aesir, it meant acceptance of fate and the fortitude to struggle on.

Ragnarok means "fate of the gods," or it is also read as the "twilight of the gods." By extension, what happened to the gods also happened to the Vikings, so they also saw Ragnarok as the "end of mankind."

When Ragnarok would be was up to the Norns to decide. As with their runic magic, the Norns would most likely have written the unfolding on the trunk of Yggdrasil, which may have been why Odin was so obsessed with acquiring wisdom and knowledge. It could also be why he was willing to hang from the World Tree for nine days and nights by his own spear so he may gain insight to see Ragnarok coming.

Here is the sequence of events:

The Great Winter, the Fimbulvetr

It was prophesied that there would come a great winter. This winter, the Fimbulvetr, would be unlike any winter ever seen before. It would last three times as long as a normal winter, and the seasons would stop changing. Thus, the realms would be covered in snow and ice for many, many months. This would cause starvation and hunger on Midgard, leaving the Norsemen to face famine.

With life-saving resources placed under strain, the world would turn to chaos as people struggle to survive, brother turning against brother in the battle for food, warmth, and medicines. Moral codes will perish before the bodies do. It shall be an age of swords and of axes. Kin will turn against kin and all that will matter is survival.

Desperation and Warnings

Fjalar, the red rooster, would crow in the forest of Gálgviðr in Jotunheim, warning the giants that the end had come. A golden rooster Gullinkambi would crow in Valhalla, warning the gods that Ragnarok had arrived, while a soot-red cock would crow in Hel's halls in Helheim, waking the dead to go to war. These would be forewarnings that would follow soon after the slaying of Baldur.

In Helheim, the great hellhound Garmr, upon hearing the rooster crowing, would begin to growl without end, eventually breaking free from his chains in a cave called Gnipahellir. It is somewhat ambiguous in the *Poetic Edda* whether the hellhound is Garmr or Fenrir, which had been chained up by the gods.

When the two mythical wolves, Sköll and Hati (meaning: one who mocks and one who hates), catch their prey, the sun and the moon would disappear from the sky. The stars would cease shining in the dark sky, and the land would know a second darkness. Heimdall would blow deeply into the Gjallarhorn, warning the gods of impending doom, and Yggdrasil would shudder with terror, shaking its leaves. As a result, mountains would crumble, and entire forests of trees would be uprooted, crashing on the icy land.

Wolves and Monsters

In the distant cave where Fenrir had been chained, the earthquakes would tear loose the unbreakable chain, freeing the great wolf. He would run forth across the land with his upper jaw scraping the clouds and the lower jaw digging up the earth, and he would swallow everything that came in his path.

The sea serpent Jormungand would spew forth poison, polluting the skies, the seas, and the land. There would be massive flooding due to the serpent's endless churning in the deep waters.

The Ship Naglfar

Jormungand would writhe in the seas, sending up such waves and tsunamis that the great ship Naglfar (meaning: nail ship) would be loosened from the place where it had been docked. This dreaded ship, which is made from the toenails and fingernails of the dead is destined to carry a terrible crew and cargo: giants, monsters, and a captain with hate in his heart—Loki.

Chaos and destruction would follow this army of giants wherever they go, and they would sail straight for Asgard with one intention in their minds: to slay the gods and burn the kingdom of the Aesir.

During the initial stages of the battle, the sky would be torn open and the fire giants would emerge from Muspelheim. These giants are said to be led by Surt who wields a burning sword. The giants would begin their march across the Bifröst as Heimdall continues to sound the alarm on Gjallarhorn.

Heimdall's Trumpet and the Battle

Despite knowing the outcome of the battle, the gods would still remain resolute and gear up for combat. The battle is almost scripted, but still the gods, giants, and the dead would play their parts to the full. Odin consults with the head of Mimir, but it seems there is no wise counsel on this day, and the gods would march out onto the field of battle.

Heimdall's horn would now play a specific melody, which can reach all the way to Valhalla. This sound would raise the dead, bringing them to life. In a final act of courage, Odin leads his einherjar, the fallen warriors he had kept and trained in Valhalla over the eons.

The gods meet their enemies on the plain called Vigrid (meaning: plain where battle surges), and there will be no mercy shown. While Odin and his magnificent warriors fight with the ferocity no previous army has ever shown, the dreaded Fenrir would swallow them whole, ending the illustrious life of Odin one-eye, the Allfather. Odin's son Vidar, blinded by a rage that may have been the berserker rage or battle fury, would rush into the fight, slashing at the beast.

As legend tells, Vidar will be wearing a special shoe made from all the scraps of leather ever discarded by every shoemaker ever to live, and he would use this thick and padded shoe to hold the jaws of Fenrir open as he stabs down into the beast's throat. Finishing off the giant wolf, he would stab the beast through the heart with his spear, thus avenging his father's death.

Garmr, Hel's hellhound, is destined to be slain by Tyr, though Tyr will perish in the fight. And Heimdall and Loki are to square off for a final combat that would see them slay each other. Thus, the watchman would finally slay the trickster.

Freyr will face the giant Surt, but since he had given up his magical sword that could fight on its own, Freyr will be sorely pushed in the combat, and in the end, he and Surt will also slay each other. Lastly, Thor and Jormungand will face each other in a final battle, and while Thor will slay the serpent with his lightning-wielding hammer, Mjöllnir, the serpent will have sprayed forth such poison as to cover Thor with the toxic fluid. Legend has it that Thor will walk nine steps after the serpent stops twitching before falling dead himself.

And so, the gods are destined to have fallen, with a few exceptions, all perishing in the great battle of Ragnarok. The destruction would still not be complete, though.

The Aftermath

Following the battle, the World Tree and all nine the realms would sink into the great seas, leaving nothing but a void, same as it had been at the beginning. One may think of this as a massive reset on the scale of the cosmos.

While some believe that this will be the ultimate end of all things, others hold that a new and verdant world will rise from the oceans again. Some of the gods would have survived the battle of Ragnarok, specifically Vidar, Vali, Modi, and Magni (Thor's sons). Other gods would be resurrected, with Hodr and Baldur also rising from the underworld.

One man and a woman, Lif and Lífþrasir (meaning: life and striving after life) would have survived Ragnarok too. They are destined to be the father and mother of the new human race in this new world. A new sun (daughter to the old one) would rise in the sky, and finally, everything would be ruled by one new and almighty ruler, whose identity is not specified.

There are two main and conflicting interpretations of the Ragnarok myth. One version seems to indicate there is no rebirth and with Ragnarok everything ends, nobody survives (McCoy, n.d.-e). In another, there is rebirth and new life, which may have been more inspired by the early Christians arriving in the Scandinavian countries. Certainly, there is quite a bit of similarity between Ragnarok's interpretations and the Christian concepts of Armageddon and also from the life of Christ.

For starters, there are a few similar symbols being used, and it makes for an interesting comparison:

Christ is nailed to a stake, and a spear is used to ultimately kill Him. Odin was hung on the World Tree, and he had impaled himself on his own spear. Three roosters announce the coming of Ragnarok, while in the Bible, the rooster crows three times to remind Peter of his betrayal.

The first time the earth ended in the Old Testament with a great flood. Ragnarok also involved serious flooding. During Ragnarok the mountains were uprooted, and in the book of Revelations, the mountains also crumble and fall into the sea.

What can we as modern day people learn from the myths and glorious stories of the Vikings? Is there some value that is contained in these beliefs that echo down the ages to enrich our lives, even in the age of technological and microscopical monsters? Indeed, there is one value I think is really valuable: to embrace fate and never lose hope.

The Norse gods knew they were destined to die. Yet, they lived each day as if they would have many more but still valued it for being precious. And on the final day, when the roosters crowed and Heimdall's great horn sang its song, they dressed in their best battle armor and they strode onto the field with courage, honor, and a spirit aimed at noble deeds. There is no use in cowering in a hole. Our fates were already written eons ago, and it's up to us to live it with the valor of the gods.

Whether your battlefield is at work, in your school, out in your town or city, or in your own home, you have the choice to cower or tower. By Thor's hammer, I hope you choose the right option.

Chapter 9:

The Norse Gods Today

Thank you for going on the journey through the Norse gods, their wars, victories, and beliefs with this book. But our journey is not quite over. Perhaps it will never be over? There is some debate on whether Ragnarok has already happened or whether it is still destined to happen. Are the gods real or simply figments of the imagination of a "primitive" culture? If the gods are real, are they still around today? What did the implications of Norse mythology look like for the early Vikings, and what does it look like today? This chapter will answer the last lingering questions you may have, so join me on the rainbow bridge one last time.

Are the Norse Gods Still Smiling Down on Midgard Today?

When wondering if the Norse religious practices (or any pagan beliefs for that matter) are still hale and whole in Northern Europe, I came across the religion Ásatrú, which is a type of neo-Viking faith (which combines Norse and Celtic traditions). It is a revival of many of the same beliefs that these Norse ancestors had during the Viking era.

Ásatrú means "Aesir faith." In 1972, it was recognized as a religion in Iceland with the authority to marry couples or officiate burials. So, perhaps the old Norse gods are still smiling down on Midgard if their faithful are still here? But how does one believe in ancient stories when you've had a modern upbringing? How can you see Odin in the ravens that fly over the forests if you "know" they are just birds and not Hugin and Munin?

The answer is that Ásatrú is there to support its followers through the trials of life by focusing on the natural world (which the gods were so deeply intertwined in) and by being mindful of the characteristics the gods embodied. So, those who follow Ásatrú cultivate honor, bravery, courage, and acceptance, and they develop a deeper understanding and respect for the myths that shaped the Norse countries so fiercely.

The Ásatrú followers celebrate festive days or holidays that are closely tied to the ancient Aesir and Vanir gods. Sacrifices are made at four public dates of the year, celebrating the solstices and equinoxes:

- Freya is honored at winter solstice with Jólablót (Yule-blót), which means to make a sacrifice or offering to Freya at this time. Appropriate offerings would include food (such as goat's meat), mead, and sacred objects such as pendants.

- Freyr is honored with the spring equinox, Sigurblót (Victory-blót). Here, spring foods such as lamb and green veggies as well mead is offered to the god of fertility.

- Humans (and their ancestors) are honored by Þingblót (Þing/assembly-blót) on the summer solstice. This is also the harvest festival, and the fertility gods are also thanked and sacrifices are made to them.

- On the first day of winter, Veturnáttablót (wintery nights-blot), the faithful turn to Odin, the wise Allfather, whom they honor with gifts and sacrifices of sacred charms, mead, and offerings of food.

There are other forms of Norse religions that are also thriving in Northern Europe and across the world, including Odinism, Heathenry, and Germanic neo-Paganism. Followers of these ways scrutinize the ancient texts such as the *Poetic Edda* to formulate their beliefs. The gods of Asgard have definitely not died yet. These polytheistic religions have assigned slightly different roles to the main Norse gods, indicating how belief can change religion and the other way around too. For these Pagans:

Odin: The ruler of Valhalla, god of poetry and riches

Thor: Sky ruler who watches over all, and he's the god of community

Freyr: Still the god of fertility

Freyja (Freya): Now the goddess of love and beauty. She is now married to Thor.

These new forms of Norse Paganism are more flexible than mainstream religions, which makes them very appealing to the growing number of people (worldwide) who are beginning to integrate Paganism into their lives. Some Pagans combine aspects of Christianity with Paganism, living a smoothly blended religious life. If it works for them, who's to say it is wrong? I discovered that while any journey into Norse mythology may seem like a history project, it is a lively and vital process, and care needs to be taken as this "history" is still very much alive for a great number of people who live in the very places where the Norse beliefs began.

The Sacred Sites

There are a number of sacred sites scattered throughout Northern Europe that are particularly motivated by Norse beliefs and myths.

Helgafell, Iceland

In Iceland, we find the breathtaking view from Helgafell (meaning: holy mountain), which is traditionally believed to provide a view into Valhalla. In the ancient times, those nearing their end would climb to the top of this rocky outcropping and look across at Valhalla. This vantage point located on the Snæfellsnes peninsula, is said to be a place of great magic where, if you follow three ancient rules, you could make a wish and have it come true. The rules were to not look back as you climbed, the walk must be made in utter silence, and the nature of their wish can never be made known to anyone else.

Lofoten Islands, Northern Norway

This is the ideal place to view the Northern Lights from. There were many beliefs surrounding the rainbow-colored lights in the sky, and some of the ancient Norsemen believed the colors were reflected from the Valkyrie's armor, while others held that it was the colors of the Bifröst, the rainbow bridge between Midgard and Asgard. Whichever belief you hold to, it is still a magnificent view to behold and well worth the trip.

Gamla Uppsala

Located just outside the city of Uppsala in Sweden, this archeological site is sure to help you dig deep to your own Viking roots. The three giant mounds at Gamla Uppsala are said to be the funeral mounds of the three

Norse gods, Odin, Thor, and Freyr. These impressively large mounds of earth definitely offer fuel for the imagination, and when I had the opportunity to visit this site, I could just imagine the three mighty gods lying there after the battle of Ragnarok.

The Rök Runestone

You can find this awe-inspiring stone in Östergötland, Sweden. While it was out in the open air and rugged landscape during the Viking days, the stone with its impressive display of runes is now housed inside a museum and is kept under roof to preserve the rune carvings. There are 760 characters of runes carved on the stone, telling riddles in poem form, which contribute to our knowledge of the Viking age. Standing before the large stone, one is struck by the sheer effort that was taken to carve the runes into the pitted surface. The Norse certainly lived a very different life from what we enjoy today, yet some of their beliefs still echo throughout our societies even now.

Norse Mythology and Popular Culture

When you hear a sentence with Norse mythology and popular culture in it, you would be forgiven for instantly thinking of the latest edition of Marvell's Thor or the Avengers. After all, we have been almost indoctrinated by the blonde hero with his large arms saving the day on the blue screen. However, Norse mythology has had an impact on popular culture long before Hollywood or the first comics caught wind of the Aesir gods.

The Norse gods have appeared in poetry, art, and song since before the more recent interpretations. Here are a few interesting takes to consider for a complete view of modern day Norse Paganism and popular culture:

Books

- *The Ballad of the White Horse* (1911) by G. K. Chesterton

This book, written at the turn of the century, highlighted the Norse gods as being false gods, pushing the reader towards Christianity, but it is an interesting take on the gods from a Christian perspective. It also makes one a little more sensitive to Snorri Sturluson's *Poetic* or *Prose Edda*, which might be equally biased.

- *The Incomplete Enchanter* (1941) by L. Sprague de Camp

Only a mere three decades after the first example, we are already finding a much more "interested" version of literature involving the Norse gods. Given the rich detail and bold characters of the gods, they are the stuff of dreams and imagination, driving a primal sense in humans.

- *The Hobbit (1937)* and *The Lord of the Rings* (1954) by R.R. Tolkien

These iconic books were admittedly inspired by the Norse gods and the realms of Yggdrasil. Gandalf is surely an interpretive version of Odin, with the elves and dwarves clearly seeming Norse in nature.

- *Life, the Universe and Everything* (1982) by Douglas Adams

Combining science fiction with myth, fantastical worlds, beliefs, and adventures unfold involving Odin and Thor.

Poetry

- William Morris' poems such as *Sigurd the Volsung*
- Seamus Heaney (1999) wrote a great translation of the ancient Norse-inspired poem *Beowulf.*

Music and Song

- German composer Richard Wagner created the four operas that make up *Der Ring des Nibelungen* based on Norse characters.
- An assortment of Viking inspired metal bands such as Manowar, Unleashed, and Kampfar.

Movies

- *Vikings* by the History Channel
- *Thor* and *the Avengers* (and a slew of other Marvel productions)

- *Erik the Viking* (which provides a humorous take on the Norse mythologies)
- *The 13th Warrior*

Other

There are many other media that we find Norse mythology making a serious mark on, from comics and manga to role-player games like "God of War." Norse mythology is not dead at all, and perhaps this is where the resurrection that came after Ragnarok has really happened? Either way, Norse mythology is certainly interesting, enriching, and entertaining.

Modern Day Impact of Norse Mythology on Scandinavia and the Viking Countries

- **The Countries**

For the people living in the countries where the ancient Vikings once did battle and built their long homes, Norse mythology will always be alive and all around them. It's seen and remembered in the names of places, the shape of the land, and a rich cultural undertone that is present in the different peoples of Northern Europe and the British Isles.

The traditions of the Vikings and Norse mythology deeply influenced the cultures and pastimes of these different lands. Viking culture is one of diversity, and the people of these countries have developed a different way of seeing the land, valuing sacred sites, and also creating a unique way of thinking.

- **Way of Living**

Many of the people living in the countries where Viking culture survives still practice similar habits, sports, and activities that the ancient Vikings would do.

- **Combining Norse Mythology and Christianity**

As mentioned, neo-Norse or neo-Paganism has evolved to include Norse beliefs and Celtic beliefs and also some Christian beliefs. There are also many similarities between Christianity and some of the tales of Norse mythology, which make for an interesting cross-reference discussion. The two religions aren't mutually exclusive, and in embracing differences and historical richness, thousands of Norse followers are able to successfully live their lives as both Christians and Pagans.

- **Tourism**

A final impact of Norse mythology is the massive market in tourism this has created in the countries where the Vikings lived such as Sweden, Denmark, Norway, Iceland, and the assortment of islands in the Baltic sea. Thousands of visitors stream to these areas to see the rune stones, enter the remains of longhouses, take modern day reconstructed tours, and visit Viking villages. Museums faithfully house texts, artifacts, and treasures of the ancient Norse times.

With the increased interest over the last 100 years, Norse mythology is again alive and thriving. The gods walk among the mortals once more as Midgard continues to thrive with its toes in the rich history of the Vikings.

Chapter 10:

Glossary

No book on Norse mythology would be complete without a glossary, and this one is a bonus with the phonetic pronunciation of these Old Norse words included so you can grr and oooo with the ancient Vikings and really get a feel for the beautiful language that is still spoken in a modern form today in parts of Northern Europe. Enjoy!

~~~~~//~~~~~

Aesir: /**ey**-seer, **ey**-zeer/ collective noun for the gods of Asgard

Alfheim: /**alf**-heym/ home of the elves

Allsherjargoði: /**als**-her-jar-koi-thee/ a high priest

Angrboda: /**ahng**-ger-boh-duh/ she who bodes anguish, the giantess that Loki had three children with, namely Jormungand, Hel, and Fenrir

Ásatrú: /**a**-sa-tru, **ow**-sa-tru/ new religion in Iceland that combines Norse and Celtic beliefs

Asgard: /**ahs**-gahrd, **as**-gahrd/ home of the gods and goddesses

Ask: /ask, ahsk/ the first man made by the gods

Bifröst: /**be**-vrast/ the rainbow bridge that connects the Nine Realms within the World Tree

Blodughofi: /**blew**-ew-gla-fee/ meaning blood hoof, it was the magical horse that Freyr rode

Blót: /bloth/ sacrifice

Brísingamen: /**bree**-sing-ah-men, bree-seen-**gah**-men/ Freya's gleaming torc

Darraðarljóð: /**dar**-ra-tharl-yoth/ Ancient rune poem found on the Rök runestone in Östergötland, Sweden, containing the tale of 12 Valkyrie plotting the deaths of warriors

Draupnir: /**draop**-neer, **drao**-pnihr/ Odin's magical ring that made eight new rings every nine nights

Dwarves: created from the maggots that lived in Ymir's corpse

Eir: /er/ handmaiden to Frigg, she was venerated as a goddess of healing

Embla: /**em**-blah, **em**-bla/ the first woman made by the gods

Fehu: /**fey**-who/ name for the phoneme "F," meaning: cattle

Fenrir: /**fen**-reer, **fehn**-reer/ marsh-dweller, the huge wolf that would swallow Odin whole

Fimbulvetr: /**fim**-bul-vin-ter/ the great winter that would come at the start of Ragnarok

Fólkvangr: /**folk**-vang-uhr/ field of the host or place of the dead

Freya (word only): /**frey**-uh/ meaning: lady

Freya: /**frey**-uh/ Freya, goddess of fertility

Freyr (word only): /freyr/ means lord

Freyr: /freyr/ Freyr, the god of fertility

Fylgja: /**filg**-ya/ the attendant spirit, the part of your psyche that is associated with your animal familiars such as Odin and his ravens

Germanic runes: the carvings on rocks that symbolizes the ideas or concepts of Norse writing

Ginnungagap: /**gin**-oong-gah-**gahp**/ the bottomless abyss that existed prior to the creation of the cosmos and into which the cosmos will collapse once again

Gjallarhorn: /**yahl-**lahr-hawrn/ the great horn of Heimdallr, which will signal the start of Ragnarok

Gothi: /**gho**-thi/ traditional Norse priest

Gullinborsti: /**goo**-lin-burst-ee/ the golden boar made by the dwarves

Gullinkambi: /**goo**-lin-kam-bee/ the golden rooster that will announce to the hall of Valhalla the start of Ragnarok

Gungnir: /**goong**-near/ Odin's spear

Hamingja:/**hahm**-ing-ya/ the talent you possess that is unique, such as Thor's battle strength

Hamr: /**ham**-er/ skin or shapeshifting potential of the self

Hati: /**hat**-ee/ a magical wolf who chases the moon and the sun

Heiðr: /**high**-thur/ meaning: bright, this was the disguise Freya assumed when she traveled the Nine Realms before the Aesir-Vanir war

Heil: /hayl/ be healthy and happy (traditional greeting)

Heil Og Sael: /**hayl**-og-sa-el/ be healthy and happy, a traditional Viking farewell

Hel: /hel/ meaning: to be hidden

Helgafell: /**hel**-gha-fell/ small mountain in the Snæfellsnes Peninsula of Iceland, meaning: holy mountain

Helheim: /**hel**-haym/ the realm that is hidden, the underworld

Himinbjörg: /**he**-min-bjohrg/ meaning: sky cliffs, it's the realm ruled by Heimdallr, who guards the Bifröst

Hliðskjálf: the seat of Odin from where he could see into all Nine Realms

Hringhorni: /**hlith**-sky-ahlf/ ship with a circle at the stern

Hugr: /**hoo**-guhr/ thought or thinking, the mind

Hvergelmir: /**hvel**-guh-mihr/ the oldest fountain in Niflheim, meaning: bubbling and boiling spring

Járngreipr: /**yarn**-greypr/ meaning: iron grippers, the iron gloves that Thor wore allowed him to grip his hammer

Jormungand/Jörmungandr: /**yawr**-m*oo*n-gahnd, **yawr**-m*oo*n-gahn-dhr/ meaning: huge monster, also the serpent in the seas around Midgard

Jotunheim: /**yawr**-turn-haym/ home of the giants

Jötnar: /**jot**-nar/ frost giants

Lif: /leaf/ meaning: life, last remaining man after Ragnarok

Lífþrasir: /**leaf**-thrass-ear/ meaning: striving after life, the last woman remaining after Ragnarok

Lokasenna: /**lok**-kah-sen-nah/ a poem from the *Poetic Edda* that features Loki's taunting of the gods. Also known as Loki's Truth

Loki: /**low**-key, **lock**-ee/ meaning: fire, knot, or spider as a quite apt translation of the trickster god's name

Megingjörd: /**mee**-ying-jorth/ the belt Thor wore, meaning: belt of power

Mimir: /**mee**-mere/ shadowy being who watches over the Well of Urd and counsels Odin

Mjöllnir: /**mee**-ol-neer/ Thor's hammer, made by the dwarves

Múspell: /**moo**-spell/ the giant who rules Muspelheim and will attack Niflheim during Ragnarok

Muspelheim: /**moo**-spell-haym/ the homeland of elemental fire, the world of Múspell

Naglfar: /**nah**-ghl-far/ a ship made of toenails and fingernails of the dead, which carries the giant army to Asgard

Nidhug: /**need**-hawg/ fierce dragon that protects the spring in Niflheim

Niflheim: /**niff**-el-haym/ the homeland of elemental ice, world of fog

Noatun: /**no**-ah-toon/ castle by the sea where Njord dwelled

Norns: /norns/ magical female beings who rule the fates of men

Norse: Germanic peoples, their beliefs, myths, culture, traditions, etc.

Northern Lights: an atmospheric phenomenon in the northernmost parts of Europe where the sky is colored with rainbow light due to light refraction from ice crystals, said to be the Valkyrie's armor or the Bifröst bridge

Poetic Edda: a collection of poems, which records most of the known knowledge about the Norse gods and their mythical adventures and journeys, by the Icelandic poet Snorri Sturluson

Ragnarok: /**rag**-na-rock/ the end of the world, the twilight of the gods, and the fate of the gods

Rök: /rock/ meaning: a skittle shaped stone or smoke

Seidr: /**say**-der/ Norse magic

Sessrúmnir: /**ses**-room-neer/ Freya's seat hall

Skadi: /**skath**-ee, **shah**-dee/ daughter of Thjazi, who had kidnapped Idun, and she later married Njord

Skalds: /skalds/ highly revered bards and poets

Skidbladnir: /**skid**-bood-nere/ magical ship that the dwarves made which could fold up to fit in your pocket

Skipta hömum: /skipta-haw-moon/ to change one's skin or transform into a different shape

Sköll: /sk-**oll**/ one who mocks, a wolf that chases the moon and the sun

Skuld: /skoold/ meaning: something that will become, the last of the Norns

Sleipnir: /**slayp**-near/ Odin's magical horse that had eight legs and was born from Loki's tryst with a magical stallion

Surt: /soort/ the fire giant who would fight against Freyr, dying by his hand and also killing Freyr

Svadilfari: /**svadil**-far-i/ the stallion who worked with the giant to build Asgard's wall and had a colt with Loki

Svartalfheim: /**swart**-ahlf-haym, **svart**-ahlf-haym/ home of the dwarves

Thialfi: /**thee**-ahlf-ee/ the human boy who journeyed with Thor and Loki

Thjazi: /**thee**-a-tsee/ giant who kidnapped Idun

Thökk: /thawk/ the old giantess who refused to weep tears for Baldur (Loki in disguise), meaning: thanks

Thrym: /threem/ meaning: noisy, the giant who stole Thor's hammer

Thrymheim: /**thraym**-haym/ home of Skadi and Thjazi

Thurisaz: /**thoo**-ri-sats/ name of the phoneme "th," which means being formed right now, the second Norn

Vigrid: /**wee**-grid/ plain where the final battle of Ragnarok will happen, meaning: giant

Til Árs ok Friðar: /til-aars-ok-fri-thar/ a good year and peace (traditional new year's wish)

Urd: /oord/ meaning: the past, the first of the Norns

Urðr: /oor-thr/ fate or destiny (also called wyrd)

Valhalla: /**varl**-hah-lah/ the hall for the brave dead, ruled by Odin

Valkyrie: /**val**-ki-ree, **varl**-koo-ree/ meaning: those who choose the new spirits, the female spirits who chose the fallen to bear to Odin's hall

Vanaheim: /**vana**-haym/ home of the Vanir

Vanir: /**varn**-eer/ the gods of Vanaheim, enemies of Asgard until the unification

Verdandi: /**ver**-dan-dee, **wer**-dan-dee/ meaning: that which is happening

Viking Age: spanned from around 793 to 1066

Völuspá: /**waw-lu**-spa/ first and best-known poem of the *Edda*

Völva: /**waw**-wa/ poem from the *Poetic Edda* that refers to the end of the gods, a practicing seidr sorceress or witch

Yggdrasil:/**eeg**-drass-ill/ the World Tree that all realms exist within

Ymir: /**ee**-mir or **y**-mir/ the first of the giants, source of all other giants

Heil Og Sæl!

Viking history and myth presents a rich opportunity to look into the past and learn for the future. It is so wildly popular that the myths, gods, monsters, beliefs, and culture now appear in movies, miniseries, games, online role-playing games (RPG), and the religious beliefs in the Norse gods are still very much alive and well today. There are even online shrines and worship sites, and there are also many conferences that strive to keep the ancient Norse culture alive and vital to many new generations of "Midgardians."

Yet, culture is never static, and those who participate in it and keep it alive also serve to change it. Much of modern day Norse mythology and beliefs have been somewhat changed by the impact of technology, new ideas, and cross pollination of other cultures and religious beliefs. This is not a new concept though, as the same happened in ancient times when one culture met a new culture. In fact, the ancient Norse traditions have definitely been changed by the influence of the beliefs of Christianity that entered Northern Europe.

As such, I keep a mental pot of salt with me when I read about the Vikings, their myths, their beliefs, and their traditions. I have to pinch myself and remember that what I read may not have been captured 100% accurately from how it happened in ancient Norse times. But I hope this book has given you an authentic taste of true Norse mythology, the mystery, history, and culture of the Vikings. More than that, I also hope you can see how that mythology is all around us today in the books we read, the movies we watch, the music we listen to, and the poems we live by.

From the skalds to the Valkyrie, from the runes to the Nine Realms, and from the gods to the giants, there is always something exciting and thought-provoking to be learned from Norse mythology. We may not be able to imagine quite what a traditional Viking's life was like, but with these stories and the wonderfully rich characters of the gods and mythical figures, we can gain some small glimpse into the past.

How I would love to climb into a time machine, travel back to those cold and frosty days, see the Scandinavian coast, and experience Viking culture first hand! For now, I content myself with books, stories, new translations, and exciting archeological finds.

So, I hope you have enjoyed these stories, my insights into the Viking culture and Norse mythology, and the trip down my own Bifröst to learn about the Vikings and their gods. Here, I leave you at the end of this book, though there will be many more adventures, discoveries, and great insights to come and these will help you understand your own beliefs even better.

Heil og sæl! Be healthy and happy!

If you have enjoyed reading this book as much as I enjoyed writing it, then I would ask for a favorable review on Amazon that other wanderers may find their way to Yggdrasil too and drain a horn of mead in the golden hall of Valhalla, where the brave shall live forever.

References

Apel, T. (n.d.). *Freyr.* Mythopedia. https://mythopedia.com/norse-mythology/gods/freyr/

Brown, N. M. (2012). *Seven Norse Myths We Wouldn't Have Without Snorri: Part V.* Norse Mythology. https://www.tor.com/2012/12/10/seven-norse-myths-we-wouldnt-have-without-snorri-part-v/

Campbell, J. (1904). *The power of myth, with Bill Moyers, p. 11.* Anchor Books.

Dronke, U. (Trans.) (1997). *The Poetic Edda: Volume II: Mythological Poems.* Oxford University

Elderberg, J. (2015). *Viking mythology: what a man can learn from Odin.* Art of Manliness. https://www.artofmanliness.com/articles/viking-mythology-odin/

Geller, P. (2016). *Frigg.* Mythology.net. https://mythology.net/norse/norse-gods/frigg/

McCoy, D. (n.d.-a). *Who were the historical Vikings?* Norse Mythology. https://norse-mythology.org/who-were-the-historical-vikings/

McCoy, D. (n.d.-b). *Odin.* Norse Mythology. https://norse-mythology.org/gods-and-creatures/the-aesir-gods-and-goddesses/odin/

McCoy, D. (n.d.-c). *Tyr.* Norse Mythology. https://norse-mythology.org/gods-and-creatures/the-aesir-gods-and-goddesses/tyr/

McCoy, D. (n.d.-d). *Vili and Ve.* Norse Mythology. https://norse-mythology.org/vili-ve/

McCoy, D. (n.d.-e). *Ragnarok.* Norse Mythology. https://norse-mythology.org/tales/ragnarok/

North, R. (2010). *The longman anthology of old English, old Icelandic, and Anglo-Norman literatures* (R. North, Trans.). Routledge. (Original Work, 13th Century).

Rach, J. (2018). *Couple exchange vows in a Viking wedding on the shores of a Norwegian lake inspired by a 10th-century ceremony – complete with longboats, a pagan priest and blood offerings.* Mail Online. https://www.dailymail.co.uk/femail/article-6129259/Couple-tie-knot-Viking-wedding-nearly-1-000-years.html

Skjalden. (2020). *Vanir.* Nordic Culture. https://skjalden.com/vanir/

The Skalds Circle. (n.d.). *The marriage of Njord and Skadi (Norse mythology)*. The skalds circle. https://theskaldscircle.com/norse-mythology/the-marriage-of-njord-and-skadi-norse-mythology/

List of Illustrations

Image 1: WikiImages from Pixabay. https://pixabay.com/photos/europe-map-1923-country-breakdown-63026/

Image 2: Yuriy Chemerys on Unsplash. https://unsplash.com/photos/pmCGouQQgFY

Image 3: ella peebles on Unsplash. https://unsplash.com/photos/kUkqoqwY61s

Image 4: Jeremy Bishop on Unsplash. https://unsplash.com/photos/EwKXn5CapA4

Image 5: LoggaWiggler from Pixabay. https://pixabay.com/photos/ervin-ahmad-lóránth-sculpture-giant-522837/

Image 6: Russo self-designed image.

Image 7: Jonas Friese on Unsplash. https://unsplash.com/photos/pS_S00R9_6I

Image 8: Russo self-designed image.

Image 9: Victor B on Unsplash. https://unsplash.com/photos/IYyvakvhi7I

Image 11: Husein Bahr on Unsplash. https://unsplash.com/photos/93afVrqOOyo

Image 12: ANIRUDH on Unsplash. https://unsplash.com/photos/8pgK7WMSnXs

Image 13: Steven Erixon on Unsplash. https://unsplash.com/photos/1xZzYbasToM

Image 14: Russo self-designed image.

Image 15: Enrique Meseguer from Pixabay. https://pixabay.com/illustrations/woman-female-warrior-hooded-2856014/

Image 16: Russo self-designed image.

Image 17: Russo self-designed image.

Image 18: Kristijan Arsov on Unsplash. https://unsplash.com/photos/tcw3nwoAgvs

Image 19: Image by Deedster from Pixabay.https://pixabay.com/photos/skull-decoration-halloween-spooky-1626803/

Image 20: Russo self-designed image.

Uncovering Greek Mythology

A Beginner's Guide into the World of Greek Gods and Goddesses

Introduction

For all the remarkable and awe-inspiring traits that make us humans who we are, the single most impressive is our ability to explain the world around us through story and pass that information down through subsequent, surviving generations. The tall tale, the caught fish which grows as large as the arms can spread, and even the fable all contribute to an ever-increasing wealth of knowledge that connects us through time and space as a disjointed but unified people. It is through common elements of story that we build a culture, religion, and society, and none of the above had a greater impact on the Western world than the Ancient Greeks.

Additionally, nothing has had a more significant impact upon the telling and codifying of stories than the written word, of which the Greeks claim the oldest surviving language in the Western world. The Sumerian language in ancient Mesopotamia, to be clear, lays claim to the title of "oldest" written alphabetic language, but it fell into disuse sometime after the third millennium BCE. Through the arrangement of their alphabet into syllables and words, the Ancient Greeks forged a series of explanations about the world that are still alive and breathing today. They are still full of wonder and power, allowing us as readers a glimpse into the minds, hearts, and fears of an entire people separated from us by time but not by emotion or intelligence.

The Ancient Greeks and their mythology occupy an undeniably foundational part of Western literature. Its figures and events have been alluded to and personified increasingly by each generation of writers who engage with it. The Trojan Horse, for instance, has wheeled its way from the wilderness of the Iliad into the stern, stone fortress of modern English euphemism, where it has settled into usage typically far less dramatic. We must conclude, then, that the primary reason for the survival of these texts is due to their written dissemination, and as such, we must use this fact to establish "when" we are talking about Ancient Greece and its myths.

We come to an interesting point: Specifically we must establish the factual context in dealing with works of fiction. "Ancient Greece" can be taken as a nebulous, primarily geographic area that spans from the island of Crete, south of the "fingers" of the Greek mainland and as far east as the shores of Turkey. These borders persisted up until and even into the Roman conquest of Greece and, based on archaeological evidence, most likely further back, all the way to 7000 BCE. Between those two points, leaders exchanged lands and titles, people exchanged goods and cultures, and armies exchanged bodies and blood, all of which became increasingly difficult to map without any method of documentation. As such, for the purposes of this book, we will safely pin our version of "Ancient Greece" somewhere between the two furthest historical points:

between the eighth and seventh centuries BCE, or around the first-known emergence of the writings of Homer, the great Greek poet.

Why start with Homer? Why not trace the mythology back to its roots, attempt to unearth its essences and origins, its "truth"? These are fair questions, and certainly interesting approaches to the topic, but they do not belong to the realm of the strictly historical; these questions are more at home in the realm of the archaeological. We are not concerned here with the reasons that the myths came to be, simply that they have already arrived packaged and ready for our enjoyment and admiration. In essence, our approach is not one of the botanist, concerned with how each part of the plant comprises and sustains the plant, but rather the gardener, who, with the same level of care, keeps the plants alive for the sake of the flower.

Therefore, we choose Homer as our starting point because his work marks the first instances in Ancient Greek history where the ethereal, cultic realms of Greek mythology and its writings intermingle with the realm of human affairs. We are treated at this time to the codification of demigod myths, a testament by the Greeks to both the power of the human being and the attention Mount Olympus could pay its creations. Homer's work balanced the power between mankind and those once-wrathful, omnipotent beings above and beneath the earth. By giving human reasoning and emotions to the Greek pantheon, the deities became more understood, less feared, and thus, more respected. No longer were the myths and religion of the Ancient

Greeks separated much as they once envisioned the heavens split from the earth, but at the horizon of Homer's centuries, they had merged, never again to be divided in writing.

What did our Ancient Greece look like, then? We know its borders, but as with any civilization anywhere in space or time, it is always more sophisticated and complex than marking off land on a map, particularly in the case of Ancient Greece. By Homer's time, our Greece had divided itself into many small, self-governing settlements, which emerged primarily due to the geography of the region. Comprising mountains and valleys on the mainland and chains of islands in the south, mass transportation and communication was incredibly difficult. Each community was essentially cut off from its counterparts by either peak or sea, and as such, by necessity, had to rely on self-sufficiency for survival.

There were, however, several "dominant" city-states in Greek affairs: Athens, Sparta, Thebes, and Corinth, all of whom, due to their population and geographic advantages, held a loose control over smaller states and through series of intricate alliances and treaties could call upon them in defense or times of conflict. We know Athens for its cultural and political importance as the cradle of democratic thought. Sparta for its military dominance and austerity, from which we gain the words "sparse" and "spartan," and which paved the way for the expansion of Greece's borders and, in turn, its population. With this population explosion and overcrowding of established city-states in the seventh century, new colonies were established all over the newly conquered territory of the Greek Mediterranean. Colonists founded these cities in the names of deities of the city-states from which they came, praying and sacrificing for prosperity and protection; it is a small proof that one of the binding agents of Ancient Greece was a universal religion.

By Homer's time, that religion was a complex web of intertwined meanings, interpretations, and representations; deities were no longer representative of single events or concepts, but rather shared the burden of their fellow divines. A colony of a city-state devoted to Demeter, as a hypothetical example, might share the same deity as her city-state, although the needs of the settlements might have differed significantly, thus resulting in Demeter's responsibility for the harvest as well as legal precedence. By the time the Parthenon was completed in the mid-fifth century BCE, the pantheon of Greek deities had come more and more to resemble the individual columns of Athena's palace. While each had their individual role, they served together, supporting a roof to protect their patrons from the unknown.

This is where this book comes in. There are countless sources on Greek mythology, in fact, one could devote an entire book to how these myths have changed hands and readings throughout the centuries, and I am almost positive that has been done. What this book looks to do is untangle the strings that comprise that web of divine columns and see them stand on their own. In the simplest terms, the aim is to present these deities, demigods, and creatures as they were understood and appreciated through the stories woven about them and their realms. Its intent is not to overcomplicate the myths through citation and counter-citation, but to elucidate and compress through the simplicity of organization and articulation of commonly held understandings. Ideally, the reader will walk away with questions of their own and investigate further reading about the mythologies and their impact on the Western world.

As such, this book is to serve as a foundation of knowledge as to the myths and figures of Ancient Greece and has no intention of exhausting all sources and questions. It is an introduction into the world of Greek myth. In the end, it is to serve as an appreciation of the storytelling's history, of dispelling the fear of the unknown through human and divine conflict, cooperation, and compromise. It is to help illuminate the depth and breadth of the universal comedies and tragedies that, across space and time, resonate with us because we have lived them ourselves in a sense. These are stories we must approach without searching for an objective, scientific, or even religious "truth" and instead give way to the truths they communicate human to human. Though polytheism has long since fallen out of Western religious thought and practice, I believe we must, when engaging these myths, hold some reverence for these once omnipotent and ubiquitous creations; they were sparked by the human mind, which in itself is the most powerful creative force ever known.

Chapter 1:

Remember the Titans

When delving into the world of Greek mythology, just as any religion and its texts, it is imperative to start at the beginning of the world. Who created it? How did it come into being? Why does it look like it does now? Was it always like this? These questions are particularly important in Greek mythology, as their answers serve as a basis for the emotional responses and reasons for all major Greek deities as they move through their history. One concept we must come to terms with when evaluating these stories is that omnipotence never equals contentedness or confidence. Indeed, the Greek pantheon operates in a similar fashion to the aristocratic court of Louis XIV; that is, its players move covertly, gracefully, manipulatively, and above all: jealously. We, as readers, or maybe mere mortals, cannot escape the thought that plagues us when we look at these stories: are the gods simply bored of eternal life? Perhaps yes, but as we will see when evaluating the beginnings of the Olympian pantheon, the only thing more difficult than obtaining control of the cosmos is maintaining it.

Chaos, Uranus, & Gaia

The Greek cosmos began with Gaia, the "Mother Earth," a concept which we still carry to this day, and Uranus. Before these two, Greek philosophers speculate, there was Chaos, translated as chasm or abyss, which was neither deity nor demon, though possessed qualities of both. One thinker, Pherecydes of Syros, asserted that Chaos most resembled water in that it is "something formless that can be differentiated." It has been articulated as the unified space of heaven and earth before their splitting apart, yielding our two divine entities. Interestingly, the Ancient Greeks deferred the debate regarding the world pre-creation to the realm of philosophy, not religion, and dubbed this field "cosmogony."

Some sources, like Hesiod's Theogony and Apollodorus' Bibliotheca, point to an immaculate conception of Uranus by Gaia; others, from Spartan poets to ancient Rome's Cicero in his De Natura Deorum, point to Aether as Uranus' father, who was the god of the "upper air," or the air which was breathed by the gods. Though parentage may be disputed, the important concept to take away is that both these deities exist for the ancient Greeks in a time and space before form, and are responsible, through experimentation and offspring, for bringing about shape to the otherwise shapeless world. It is not until subsequent generations of deities that we see the emergence of divinity resembling mankind, one Titan going so far as to create humanity with his own hands.

Despite not giving these original deities a specific, recognizable form, it is nonetheless important to note that the Ancient Greeks still bestowed them with personality; these divines were governed by, as we will see, something eerily close to human emotion. The early gods and their children lend us a terrific insight into Ancient Greek logic: ubiquitous as divine energy and nature was, it was always under the flawed thumb of human dominance. Though there were many mysteries surrounding the ancient world, the Greeks nevertheless positioned themselves in the very middle of it and were convinced their modes of thinking were as close to divine as any could get.

Uranus, by all accounts and despite his contested origin, is universally agreed upon, as Apollodorus writes, "the first who ruled the world." Here we see for the first time the Greeks giving preference to the sky, given Uranus' realm of the heavenly air. It could be that the sky is given this weight because of its intangibility. It could also be that the Ancient Greeks structured their physical surroundings in a simple hierarchy; naturally, the sky exists above the earth and sea, and the earth and sea above the underworld. This is a theme that will articulate itself and become more apparent throughout our whole study of Greek mythology: the domains, and thus deities, of sky and sea, perpetually dominate the realm of land due, in part, to their immense unknowable and therefore frightening qualities.

Regardless of whence he came, Uranus with Gaia produced twelve children, the Titans, who further divided up the cosmos into their realms, ranging from the expansive and concrete, such as the oceans, to the unfathomable and intricate, like time. The two had additional children who walked the earth and carried the early, grotesque marks of the human form: these were the five Cyclopes, hulking one-eyed creatures, and the three "Hecatoncheires," or the "Hundred-Handed Ones." These, as one may guess, were behemoths, unsurpassed in "size and strength" covered with one hundred hands and fifty heads. The names of these creatures the reader can search out easily enough; they are not important enough to our exploration of mythologies to delve into. Of the sets of children, those who demand our most pressing and scrutinous attention will be the twelve Titans, although it is important to set the stage for their rise via the Cyclopes and their Hundred-Handed brothers.

The human-like offspring of the two original deities were despised by Uranus, who, setting the thematic stage for many myths to come, tied together and thrust the five Cyclopes and all three "Hundred-Handed Ones" into Tartarus, the emptiness beneath the earth, a place "as distant from the earth as the earth from the sky," according to our old friend Apollodorus. Greek cosmogony points to Tartarus as below Chaos in the ancient layer cake of the world, while Chaos is below the earth. This left the twelve Titans as the sole eventual heirs of the earth and cosmos, although, as we will see, nothing could possibly be that easy, even for the divines.

Cronus & Rhea

Though there were twelve Titans, thirteen by some counts, those that concern us are Cronus, the youngest Titan and ruler of time, and Rhea, his older sister and eventual wife, the "mother of the Gods." From these two sprang the most recognizable and immortal of the ancient Greek religion; the Olympian gods and goddesses, those who live on today as the noble subjects of literature and art.

Cronus, much like his mother Gaia, has survived in concept through the ages. He is pictured in various ways and interpreted in a variety of ways; from the benevolent Father Time, sometimes at certain festive times of the year referred to as Santa Claus, to the scythe-wielding, hooded specter of death we call the Grim Reaper, Cronus is, in some sense, the only remaining true master of his ancient domain.

That he was the youngest of all twelve Titans is important to note as well. The cosmos would have been divided up according to spaces and divine objects; the oceans, the moon, and the sun all had their respective Titanic rulers, but until Cronus came to be, all was static. As the youngest of the Titans, he represents action, youthful energy, and constant change and shuffling. He is a symbol, according to many Greek and modern sources, of the bridging of gaps, of moving simultaneously toward and away objects and goals; small wonder, then, that as the mythology of the

Greeks unfolds, his appearance and aims shift considerably, as do his worship purposes.

Rhea, on the other hand, holds a place much less concrete in these stories. Aside from her role as mother of the Olympians, she has been excluded from Mount Olympus herself; the Ancient Greeks did not regard her as an Olympian in her own right for some reason. She has been cited in ancient debates regarding the origin of the Olympians as perhaps a river, and in later texts, she is determined to be the "Great Mother," upon whom depend, according to Apollodorus, "the winds, the ocean, [and] the whole earth beneath the snowy seat of Olympus." It is not too far a leap, then, to imagine Rhea occupying the ever-changing world within time, the manifest changes we witness with time's passing; every Father Time requires his Mother Nature.

But how is Rhea different from Gaia? It's a fair question to ask. Both are female representations of the planet or surrounding world; surely it is tenuous to separate them along merely hereditary lines? True, both goddesses are similar in their domains, and this may lend confusion to their roles, but one important distinction must be made: it is in the manifestations of change in the physical world that differentiates Rhea from Gaia. The latter remains the divine representation of the static, solid earth, devoid of change.

One interesting difference emerges between the parents of the Olympian deities: their forms of worship and appreciation. One can undoubtedly state that the Greek pantheon was patriarchal; the most powerful of all the divines was male, as were nearly every single demigod. However, when it came to worshipping the older, primordial divines, we find staggering evidence that Rhea enjoyed a level of cultic activity that her male counterpart did not. Across the ancient Mediterranean world, there exist ruins of temples presumably devoted to Rhea, whereas monuments and devotions to Cronus are limited to a single feast day. Perhaps this was due to the individual roles they each played through the history of Greek mythology; Cronus, as we will see, certainly lives up to his robed, skeletal persona. One should consider, though, the notion of tangibility in the appreciation and worship of Rhea.

The ancient Greek world, as we have established, was full of the unknown. What was beyond, let alone beneath the ocean, was left to the terrible toys of the mind's imagination. The same was true for the air; it was an infinite, unfathomable space. It is important to note that both domains were male-dominated in terms of mythology; not only was the earth and its personification female, but it was also the realm of the seen, the felt, and the heard, where the Greeks lived and breathed, fought and died.

What we see with the introduction of the first generation of divines is the emergence of a single theme: change. Before Cronus, Rhea, and the other pairs, the world was merely still and immobile, two distinct traits that are far removed from the human experience. Thus, we are again confronted with the notion that the Greeks infused human elements into their religion and did not let the religious elements and practices govern or justify their human counterparts.

The Dawn of the Golden Age

Despite the myriad of disagreements among mythological sources regarding the early Greek deities, one thing is certain: at some point, Cronus usurped his father Uranus' throne in the heavens through violence. This first act of destruction opened the door for all divine conspiracies to follow.

As we know, Uranus had cast several sets of his children into the depths of the earth: The Cyclopes and the Hecatoncheires, which incurred the wrath and spite of Gaia, and by some accounts, physically injured her as well. According to Hesiod's Theogony, Uranus would descend upon the earth every night, covering the world with darkness to mate with Gaia. We are told that he banished his children to Tartarus because he found them hideous and wished them never to see the light of day. Having birthed the Titans, Gaia, furious of course with Uranus for his maltreatment of his firstborn children, recruited, according to Hesiod, the "wily, youngest, and most terrible of her children," to exact revenge upon the ruthless Uranus.

Cronus, in this affair, was not entirely innocent himself; in many sources, he is cited as being either cruel, hateful toward his father, or oftentimes both. Though Gaia had initially summoned all her sons to avenge the banishment of her children, only Cronus answered the call due to his unyielding envy of Uranus' power. Equipping him with a sickle, or in some retellings, a scythe, she had fashioned from flint, she instructed the young Cronus to hide in ambush and await the nightly descent of his father. Armed with his weapon, and night having fallen, Cronus seized his opportunity and castrated his father, throwing his genitals into the sea.

The castration of Uranus yielded two interesting results. The first was that the blood from Uranus' wound, upon hitting the soil, gave rise to the race of giants, another creature like the Cyclopes and Hecatoncheires who had the physical characteristics of human beings, although the giants were notably much closer in appearance. Uranus' blood also birthed the three Furies. We can understand this in several ways. One, perhaps overly gloomy, interpretation is that violence begets humanity; those acts of great physical harm render us closer to our true selves than any pleasurable experience. Another way to look at this result is to read that change is inevitable, and if one remains complacent and overly content, time will render a person impotent, so to speak.

The second happening due to Uranus' misfortune was the emergence of the first Olympian. After Cronus had dispatched the parts into the ocean, they took to the water, creating an immense white foam. From that foam blossomed the goddess Aphrodite, who came to represent beauty, love, passion, and procreation. In separating the divine from himself, so to speak, the Greek mythos is moving ever closer toward humanity. On the one hand, we are left with the sexless body of

Uranus whose blood yields the hardened, rock-like multitudes of giants; on the other, the severed sensitive pieces swallowed up by the sensuous sea conjuring up a single presence of undying passion.

The dispatching of Uranus brought forth what Ancient Greek scholars, poets, and mythographers refer to as a "Golden Age." Cronus ruled over the entirety of the cosmos unopposed, immorality was unknown, and as such, there was no need for legal custom; those of the time were carefree, and food was in vast abundance. The Golden Age makes its appearance first in the works of Hesiod, who we have referenced before, and seems to transcend the realm of the religious or mythological, and dip slightly into the pseudo-historical. Of course, we cannot be looking into these stories as holding any historical weight, but it is intriguing to note that there was some held belief that a version of mankind existed in Cronus' Golden Age. Conceptually, perhaps the closest thing we can equate to this mythological belief is the garden of Eden, where, according to the Bible, humans were, although they behaved with the instincts of animals.

Iapetus & Clymene

It is important to note, when dealing with mythological genealogies, those important but peripheral couples whose reference early on will save excessive confusion and explanation later when discussing the myths of their children. With such fanfare arrive the Titans Iapetus and Clymene, who, as related as Cronus and Rhea, brought into being the second generation of Titans, most notably Atlas and Prometheus.

It is said that Iapetus, brother of Cronus, is responsible for the growth and multiplication of mankind, that his sons, the next Titans, bore the burden of the most wicked of humanity's traits. Indeed, this seems to be the case; we can point to the downfall of both Prometheus and Atlas as human folly, and less divine interference or wrath. Iapetus has survived, according to some scholars, all the way to the time of the Bible, where parallels have been drawn between himself and Japeth, the son of the Old Testament's Noah. We can see the similarities for ourselves in looking at both personalities; Iapetus, like Japeth, is viewed in both religious contexts as the "progenitor of mankind."

While Iapetus was a Titan of the first generation, his wife Clymene was an Oceanid, a nymph of the sea, a daughter of the Titans Oceanus and Tethys. The Oceanids were charged with the care of the young and, surprisingly, were not strictly associated with the water. Several of the Oceanids appear as rocks, trees, and even entire continents throughout Greek myth. Though they were often held in high regard, they were never elevated to the plane of deification themselves.

It seems fitting, then, that the sons of a Titan, a hulking immortal, and a decidedly undivine nymph should produce children as powerful as they were flawed. Atlas, we see pictured incessantly as the man carrying the earth upon his shoulders; a punishment passed down for his all too human transgression, which we will address in more detail in the following chapters. Alongside Prometheus, his brother, the two form what will be marked as the first evidence of physical punishment in the Greek myths, and as such, lends itself nicely to a semblance of a moral compass.

Hyperion & Theia

Hyperion and Theia, our third set of prominent Titans, owe their importance, much like Iapetus and Clymene, to their offspring. Hyperion tends to wallow in relative obscurity compared to his brothers and sisters, and indeed, extraordinarily little is known or recorded about him as far as stories are concerned. What we do know, through several ancient sources, is that he was watchful and observant, diligent in his attention, and as such, became the first entity to fully comprehend the change of seasons and the movement of time. He was revered as a god of light, watchfulness, and time, albeit in a different capacity than Cronus, who was a master of time itself. We see further movement toward the intersection of divine and human with the properties given Hyperion; to observe, comprehend, and analyze are all three very distinct human traits.

Theia's place in the pantheon seems just as opaque, unfortunately, as many of her fellow primordial goddesses and Titans. By some accounts, she occupies a similar standing as the mother of the earth, as she is addressed by Pindar in one of his many odes as "Theia of many names." She is the supposed reason mankind is fascinated with gold; because it shines and gleams by her blessing, she is regarded as a goddess of "shimmer," not of wealth or prosperity. She seems to be a perfect match for Hyperion, as one of the greatest qualities that light bestows upon anything is its glow.

Between them, they bore three children: Helion, Selene, and Eos, the sun, moon, and dawn, respectively. According to myth, across the entire cosmos, none were more admired for their beauty and chastity than these three, which, given their cosmological locations, makes sense. The sun and moon, being isolated not only from each other but from the earth as well, do strike within us even today a sense of wonder and awe.

By one account, Helios and Selene were not born as immortal sun and moon but rather became so through, as is so common in the ancient Greek mythologies, acts of jealous violence. Theia was said to have garnered the title of "Great Mother" because of her standing as the eldest female of all twelve Titans and subsequently raised her siblings as a mother might. Eventually, however, her desire for her own children and thus heirs to the cosmic throne emerged, and she took Hyperion for a husband and had her three children. Naturally, this sparked jealousy in the remaining Titans, who conspired against their brother by executing him and kidnapping Helios and drowning him in the river Eridanus. When Selene discovered what had happened to her brother, she threw herself off a roof, while Theia, in a daze, wandered the banks of the Eridanus in search of her son's body. While she was wandering, she beheld a vision of her son. He told her not to mourn the deaths of either of her children, for, in the future, vengeance would be swift and terrible for the offending Titans, and her children would be transformed into the immortal Sun and Moon. While we cannot say for certain that her children are, in fact, those two celestial bodies, we do know that the first half of Helios' prophecy is devastatingly accurate.

Chapter 2:

Dawn of the Olympians

Tracing the Greek mythologies back to their creation myths is an entangled and convoluted process. The difficulty arises in that none of the early, primordial gods had specific forms, or rather were representative of all things. In looking at source materials, the early Greek scholars, poets, and philosophers, it seems the only unsatisfactory reward for our scrutiny appears to be a shrug of those ancient, rhetorical shoulders. Those accounts which survive seem to differ; those mythological agreements those documents point to are, for the most part, nonexistent and thus exceedingly difficult to verify. Nothing seems for certain in the creation of the universe despite how confidently the mythology was taken for fact by these thinkers; the universe before the Olympians was vague and difficult to pinpoint in a series of events. As the ancient world became divided up among deities, elements within the physical world became codified and easier to explain and develop through story. In this chapter, we will see the division of the natural world further, and the movement away from the primordial deities into the realm of the familiar Olympian pantheon that is still celebrated today.

Cronus & Rhea

We begin, yet again, with our set of indispensable Titans: Cronus and Rhea. In prior myths, we saw that Cronus conspired with his mother against Uranus, his father, castrating him and removing him from power, ushering in what mythographers and poets deemed the "Golden Age." How Cronus achieved this was by imprisoning his brothers and sisters as well as the Cyclopes and "Hundred-Handed Ones," thus achieving sole possession of the realms of the universe.

In these times of peace and monarchical rule, Cronus and Rhea, much like their father and mother before them, birthed and raised several sons and daughters. Their offspring would become the core deities of the ancient Greek pantheon: Zeus, Demeter, Hera, Hestia, Poseidon, and Hades. These gods would eventually divide the world up further than their ancestors along more concrete lines, opening the door for more myth and morals, though we are getting ahead of ourselves.

To return to the Golden Age: though Cronus and Rhea controlled the known universe in times of unrivaled peace, it was prophesied by Gaia that Cronus should be overthrown by his children, much in the same way that he had overthrown his own father. Prophesy plays an immense part in Greek mythology and practice; from the earliest myths, there is a foretelling of even deities' destinies. Thus, the Greeks took the words of the oracles very seriously all over the ancient Mediterranean.

Cronus, in his wily and terrible way, was determined to deny his fate. In a cannibalistic spectacle before the unknown, he resorts to devouring his children upon their births, consuming them, and holding them within his body. What we see are a decided shift in Cronus' values and representations: in the early primordial days, he is a liberator and progenitor of his family of divines, and by the end of his Golden Age, he has come to represent stagnation, the slowing of time, and ultimate death. Here he lives up to his image as the Grim Reaper; still bearing his scythe, he is the timeless march toward the end, consuming the years and multitudes of youth.

Just as conspiratorial as her mother, Rhea could not bear witness to the destruction of her children by their father and smuggled her youngest child to the island of Crete, to the south of mainland Greece, far away from Cronus by ancient measurements. Having seen Cronus devour her first five children, she refused to allow the same fate to befall Zeus. Cleverly, she knew she would be unable to hide the birth of Zeus from Cronus, so she wrapped a stone in swaddling clothes and gave it to Cronus to consume as he had his other children. This stone became known as the Omphalos, the center, or "navel" of the world, whose mythological and literary symbolism is still conjured today. She entrusted the care of her youngest child, in some accounts, to a goat named Amalthea and a troop of armored dancers whose shouts and claps kept Cronus from discovering the young Zeus' cries. Other accounts state that Zeus was entrusted in the care of Adamanthea, a nymph who suspended Zeus by a rope between the realms of sky, earth, and sea to hide him from the all-seeing eyes of Cronus.

No matter how or under whom, Zeus grew to be a powerful, divine being, and after reaching maturity received a poison from Metis, who was one of the many sea nymph daughters of Oceanus and a representation of magical cunning. He forced it upon his father, who vomited up all the youth he had consumed, although in reverse order: first, the stone fell from his mouth, followed by his children from youngest to oldest, Poseidon to Demeter, Hestia, Hades, and Hera in between. Cronus, of course, being divine and cruel, would neither die nor abdicate, and the assault on his throne erupted into a full-scale, apocalyptic war known as the Titanomachy, which we will explore in the next section.

Looking at the first part of this myth, we are treated to the emergence of new themes and some themes we have visited before. The first, and most prevailing, is the oppression of youth, and youth's eventual and inevitable revenge. Uranus imprisoned several sets of children beneath the earth; Cronus imprisoned all his children except one within his body. Both had revenge exacted upon them by their youngest sons with the help of their mothers, which leads us to a second theme. Again, we see that although the Greek pantheon is primarily a patriarchy, divine female wisdom and input are essential to these stories. This notion carried over into practical religious worship for the Greeks, as oracles and soothsayers throughout the ancient Mediterranean were decidedly young women.

A new theme that emerges in Zeus' rise is that of the divine gift; throughout Greek mythology going forward, gifts from above are imperative to the success of heroes, particularly demigods. It is through these gifts, stemming from Metis' simple poison all the way to Perseus' winged horse, that the righteous triumph over the wretched, despite any divine-ordained odds. Through the concept of divine gift-giving, the Greeks bring themselves in their stories ever closer to their divines and bring those deities closer to the realm of the human. It also serves as a theme to justify the exploits of demigods as such, as we will see; if a human being receives an object from Mount Olympus, how could he not bear some closer resemblance to Zeus than a man who has received nothing?

Finally, what comes from this story are specific places. In the primordial eons of Uranus, there were no "locations" as we imagine or know them; the world was as nebulous as night itself, events flashing quickly within it and without context. We see that with the rise of the Olympians, the Greeks are bestowing a sense of their constructed world upon their myths; while the river which drowned young Helios was fictional, the island where Zeus was reared is rooted in the realm of fact, even if his story is symbolic.

The Titanomachy

The battle between the gods, the Titanomachy, lasted, according to Hesiod, ten years, and pitted Cronus and his old regime against his sons and daughters, known as the Olympians. After having forced his father to disgorge his siblings, Zeus set to work liberating the Cyclopes and the Hundred-Handed Ones from Tartarus so that they may help him to overthrow Cronus. Cronus called upon his Titan brothers and sisters, once so reluctant to engage in conflict, and the battle lines for the war of the fate of the cosmos had been drawn.

It is important to note that while allegiances in this war fell along generational lines, the Titans Themis and Prometheus broke rank and sided with the Olympians. Themis, for her part, was the primordial representation of order, fairness, and natural law. Prometheus, we know, is a Titan bearing human traits and flaws, and is one of the four children of Iapetus. Again, the combination of these two further bridges a gap between the human and the divine for the Ancient Greeks. We can read this choice by the two Titans as dogmatic: that it is part of the natural order of the world for human beings to side with the new natural order, or that it behooves them not to resist cosmic change.

In freeing the Cyclopes, Zeus rendered a set of allies who would ultimately bestow upon him his greatest symbol and source of his power. From their forges, the Cyclopes crafted for Zeus his everlasting symbols: the thunderbolt and lightning, weapons that would help turn the tide of the war against the Titans. Interestingly, both thunder and lightning had previously been hidden from the world by Gaia, the primordial mother. His Hundred-Handed uncles, though bound to the earth by grotesque corporeal form, hurled giant rocks and boulders toward the heavens to dislodge Cronus and his siblings.

With thunder and lightning in hand and allies on earth, Zeus unseated Cronus and the other Titans, imprisoning them deep within Tartarus in a fitting, poetically just punishment. To distribute justice further, he dictated that his Hundred-Handed uncles should guard the Titans' prison for eternity. One of Cronus' primary leaders, Atlas, brother of Prometheus, was met with special punishment. For eternity, he would be responsible for holding the world in place upon his shoulders, and we always see his image rendered so.

Dividing the Earth

Order had been restored to the cosmos after ten years of constant struggle, and the remaining task was to divide the spoils of war between the victors. All the Olympians agreed: Zeus would take control of the skies as supreme ruler, while his brothers Poseidon and Hades would claim as their territory the sea and the underworld, respectively. The earth, at which we will take a closer look, was to remain neutral ground, free to all and beyond divine interference unless deemed necessary by the Olympians.

The earth has been divided after the ten-year struggle, we can see, into three parts, and all of them are controlled by male entities. What of the Olympian sisters? In carving up the known world, they appear to be utterly neglected and shut out of sharing any potential power. While this is true in a certain sense, in other ways, the female Olympians garner more precious and potent power than all three of their male siblings combined.

The original three Olympian sisters, Hera, Hestia, and Demeter, were given realms not as concrete or even nearly as quantifiable, but rather were entrusted with entire worlds that ensured growth, happiness, and prosperity among the newly established cosmos. While the earth was to remain an essentially neutral arena to be merely observed by the divines, the nuanced domains of the three Olympian sisters almost guaranteed a direct control over its destiny. Their worlds were the intangible necessaries of mortal life: the bounty of harvest, the wooing of hearts, and the propagation of mortal species. What jumps out to the modern reader regarding the Olympian division of the world is that the aforementioned "female" domains seem to relate directly to human survival, that while there may not be direct divine "interference" upon the earth, there is a gentleness guiding it. Without these crucial pieces, the earth remains stagnant, just the same as if not worse off than the times before Cronus' Golden Age.

The Seat of the Gods

The Olympians are named for their home in the clouds, the legendary Mount Olympus. The seat of the gods is striking because it holds a tangible geographic location; it is in the eastern central part of mainland Greece. It is technically not a single mountain, but a chain of peaks, and owes its geological distinction due to its peaks' smooth, almost circular appearance, and relatively flat tops. These mountains can be, and in fact are, climbed and conquered, and countless photos and postcards bearing its image are strewn all over the modern world. There is certainly nothing mythological about the course of nature that formed this impressive range, though the ancient Mediterranean would have seen it differently.

From the Ancient Greek perspective, we can presume that the world was bordered on four sides: to the south, the inhospitable deserts of Egypt, to the west, the unfathomable ocean and the ends of the earth, to the east, the savage unknown of Persia, and to the north, the awesome heights of Mount Olympus. The Greeks presumed that between these four borders sat their country and beyond them, the world's end. The remarkable similarity between three of these four borders is that they are flat; there are no mountains atop the ocean, the closest thing resembling a peak in Egypt would be the man-made pyramids, and Ancient Persia was perched upon a plateau, which, while elevated, is essentially a plain.

As such, we are left with Greece's northern border, the fabled chain of mountains that separates it from its northern contemporaries, the Macedonians. We have already seen that the Ancient Greek world's smaller states owed their independence and self-sufficiency due to their relative geographical isolation. Is it so difficult to imagine that such ideas regarding geographic borders could expand to include an entire culture with a shared religion? Who better to protect the Greeks from the threat of their northern neighbors than the divines themselves? What could be more simultaneously intimidating for an enemy and comforting for a Greek than knowing that Zeus and his brothers and sisters were directly observing the movements of the country and simultaneously preventing any intrusion upon Greek soil?

While we do have the physical "northern border" of Mount Olympus, it seems that throughout mythology and Ancient Greek history, Mount Olympus occupies a largely symbolic space as well. In keeping with the Ancient Greek self-sufficient and geographically isolated thinking, it seems that by many accounts, "Mount Olympus" was a point of reference to every early city-state. Thessaly, for instance, had its Olympus, and Olympus existed as far outward as Cyprus. The islands of Ionia and Lesbos each claimed a Mount Olympus as well. It seems that, on the one hand, to these early states, Mount Olympus was merely the highest visible point of their surroundings. On the other hand, a culture devoted to physical representations and housings of deities as spaces of worship and protection could have seen their peaks as a sort of temple. While each city-state had its patron deity and a temple devoted to it, it is understandable that the population of a place would enjoy the security of the watchful eye of all twelve Olympians. This "together but separate" concept surfaces and resurfaces throughout the stories atop Mount Olympus as well: oftentimes, the domain of a deity, though clearly marked off and isolated, will share some conceptual heavy lifting with another divine.

The Stage is Set

We now have, in what I hope was presented concisely, accurately, and without confusion, all the necessary background information to truly begin looking at the major figures in Greek mythology. Before proceeding, however, I do believe it is important to note a few simple, philosophical evaluations regarding these stories.

Of course, we know that none of these myths or figures hold any religious sway in the current century, but they are certainly valuable literary symbols. Its believers are long gone, and all that truly remains are wind-pocked columns and edifices of once-proud temples. In analyzing these ancient stories, the reader often makes the mistake of seeking a moral conclusion, or a compass needle pointing them toward "good" and away from "evil." The Ancient Greek pantheon and its practitioners did not operate in such a capacity; these stories and figures were explanatory and taken for granted as fact; the moral compass and the roots of the universe were left to the realm of philosophy.

Mythology, then, if we can imagine it, existed in a place where science now stands; it was a method of understanding the physical world and humanity's place within it. It is a misstep to try to obtain a glimpse into the ethics of Ancient Greece through these stories; they do not hold the same textual or structural elements as later texts we equate to the religious. "But," you might be correct in asking, "haven't you already dissected several of these early creation myths to draw some governing principle from them?" I cannot deny this fact; flipping back even three pages will reveal it. Though I have and will continue to conduct a rudimentary analysis of many of these major myths going forward, I do not believe they fall into the world of moralizing. There are plenty of surviving Greek philosophical texts regarding morality, and even one of the great Greek writers, Aesop, has devoted his Fables to fundamental moral principles. However, we notice that the subject of Aesop's work is not the divine Olympians hovering over the plane of earth, but rather the animals that inhabit it, illustrating that in the eyes of the Ancient Greeks, the moral compass was a purely mortal concern.

The gods, as such, act as closely to their original oath as possible; they truly let the earth and its inhabitants govern themselves and establish a moral code befitting of their times. While they do not necessarily interfere, there are, as we will see, countless instances where they meddle, take on the form of beasts and manipulate people among other trickeries, and even turn individuals into a variety of things. It is not until we get to the epic poems of demigods that we see true intervention; however, the instances in which we see it are usually fraught with hesitation by the powers at be.

So, to conclude, in order to begin, we know the creation story of the Ancient Greek world, the basic realms inhabited by the male and female Olympians, how they are related, and that these stories are intended at their heart to explain the natural world. We see, in simple terms, how the Greeks perceived that world and how their surroundings helped give rise to the notion of security within the temple structure. We know that the further the divines divided their world, the closer they came to humanizing themselves, and as such, the closer humans came to becoming divine. We will see that gap grow even smaller with the emergence of demigods in later chapters. We have hopefully established a relatively coherent timeline of events for the creation of the cosmos and the rise of the Olympians despite differing and diverse sources scattered throughout time. We should have a basic working framework to operate within when it comes to these myths and figures of Ancient Greece, and all that remains is to dive headfirst into the stories themselves.

Chapter 3:

The Big Three

Now that we have a sketch of the roots of the broader mythological workings of the Ancient Greeks, we will change our approach going forward from a narrative perspective to a more encyclopedic one. We will be looking at deities individually and in clusters less through their interconnection through story but rather according to their importance and prevalence in the mythologies, though, of course, some overlap is bound to occur. I hope to avoid retracing previously established information as much as possible; although most myths in the Greek tradition hold more than one primary deity as characters, I will try to devote each tale to the deity who most occupies its foreground. We will start with the most visible and "legendary" deities and work our way through the pantheon to hopefully render a basic understanding of how the Greek divines operated.

Our first three we have chosen because of their ubiquity; in nearly every single myth available for the reader in the modern day, at least one of these three deities make themselves known to figures in the story as well as to the reader. These are the three major Olympians: Zeus, who we have covered briefly in the establishment of the Greek world, Hera, his wife and sister, and Poseidon, the lord of the depths of the sea. From these three come nearly all the gods and demigods to follow; they are responsible for the propagation of the Olympians and mortal Greek heroes.

Zeus

The immortal Zeus, having banished his Titan predecessors to the depths of Tartarus, presided over the Ancient Greek world as its supreme ruler from his seat on Mount Olympus. With his iconic thunderbolt, he was lord of the skies and king of all Olympians. He was, for the Greeks, a manifestation of the sky, lightning, law, and order and bears considerable resemblance to other European chief deities: the Norse Thor and Roman Jupiter, most notably. There are many more associations made with Zeus throughout religious iconography and tradition, and to go into each in detail would distract from our main ideas, but should the reader be curious, there are a multitude of texts devoted to just such a subject.

As we know, he was the youngest of all Olympians, or by some arguments the oldest, as his siblings had spent their lives in Cronus' stomach. He ultimately married his sister Hera; by some accounts, however, the two deities had begun their relationship in secret. Between the two, the pantheon ballooned in number from the small six who had snatched control of the world to a staggering 18 deities, not counting those countless demigods whom Zeus also fathered. Among his offspring, we count Ares, Hephaestus, Artemis, Apollo, and Athena, to name only a handful. His virility granted him the title of "All-Father," and was celebrated across the ancient Mediterranean as the sole representation of Greek strength, power, and religious thought. As his realm was the endless, expansive sky, any event or seemingly random occurrence that could not be attributed to a specific deity automatically fell into the hands of Zeus. In this way, his image and realm grew even more far-reaching.

Just as every region of the Greek world had their own Mount Olympus, temples to Zeus were no less common. Given his stature as king of all deities, nearly every Greek city center had a temple devoted to him, some, of course, larger than others. Fittingly enough, the center of Zeus worship, and Olympian worship in general, lay in a city called Olympia, which boasted the site of the fabled Olympic Games. The city hosted these games every four years in the name of the king of the gods, complete with animal sacrifices and feasting. One story claims that the sacrificial altar of Zeus in Olympia was carved from ash instead of stone due to the thousands of animals that had been sacrificed there.

Myths

One thing we can read about Zeus' personality through his myths is his obsession with youth and beauty, going so far as to destroy the lives of those mortals he finds attractive. We see that many of his myths are centered on the possession of the young and ideal by manipulation, force, or coercion. For example, in the myth of Europa, Zeus had become so infatuated with the eponymous Phoenician king's daughter, who was the ideal representation of mortal beauty, that he disguised himself as a virginal white bull among her herds. According to Hesiod, the bull breathed a "saffron crocus" from his mouth. Europa grew enchanted by the bull, ultimately climbing upon its back. The bull, Zeus in disguise, took off running into the ocean, whisking Europa away to the island of Crete. Zeus then reveals himself and "seduces" Europa, to put it mildly, beneath an evergreen tree. The result of their Cretan retreat was the birth of Minos, a powerful king who would lend his name to that great beast of legend: The Minotaur.

Another instance where Zeus' obsession with youth and beauty emerges is in the myth of Ganymede. Ganymede was a Trojan and, by Homer's account, another devastatingly beautiful human being. "The loveliest born," Homer dictates in his Iliad, "of the race of mortals," and of course, Zeus took notice of the young man and became infatuated. Just as with Europa, Zeus finds the youth among herds of animals and transforms himself into an animal again, albeit this time a proud, giant eagle. He abducts the boy and carries him into the sky, where he is to become the immortal cupbearer for all the gods upon Mount Olympus. Ganymede is transformed into the constellation Aquarius and is visually manifest as a cloud: that which brings water and is closest to the sky.

Our humanlike Titan, Prometheus, plays an important role in the mythology of Zeus. On one occasion, humanity offered Zeus a sacrifice of animal bones wrapped in fat instead of meat swaddled in cloth. Furious with the deception, the lord of the sky decided to withhold fire from mankind, thus thwarting its development. Through trickery and cunning, sympathetic Prometheus smuggled fire in a stalk of fennel from Olympus and bestowed it upon humanity. Of course, all-knowing Zeus discovered this treachery as well, and to punish Prometheus, he chained him to a rock where every day an eagle descended upon his body to devour his liver, which would regenerate overnight, and upon which the eagle would descend the next day again. Why Zeus chose the liver to be devoured is intriguing; according to many, the Ancient Greeks presumed the liver to be the location of all human emotion. Perhaps Prometheus is to be punished for becoming too close to mankind.

We are also given parity between Zeus and other Indo-European religious texts when it comes to the flood myth; it seems every major deity at some point must decide to wipe the slate of the earth clean. In Zeus' case, as with many other supreme beings, he had grown tired of humanity's decadence and summoned his brother Poseidon to aid in the destruction of the species via inundation. He granted mercy to one couple: Deucalion, who is the son of the perpetually half-eaten Titan Prometheus, and his wife, Pyrrha. As these stories go, the two construct an ark and eventually find solid ground at the foot of Mount Parnassus, north of Corinth near Delphi. Offering sacrifices to Zeus, the two throw "the bones of the earth," or rocks, over their shoulders, which Zeus then transforms into humans.

Hera

Hera, the eldest sister and wife of Zeus, is arguably the most ancient figure in Greek mythology; by many accounts, her presence and image in Ancient Greece predate Zeus. She is the goddess of marriage, childbirth, women, and family, and most notably surrounds herself with graceful, noble animals. The lion and peacock, to name two, are symbols often associated with Hera in Ancient Greek lore.

Images of Hera can be found all through ancient temple ruins up through contemporary literature. She, along with Zeus, was a near-ubiquitous presence in the worship centers of Greek cities; more than a representative figure, she was rendered by her marriage to Zeus as the queen of the gods. Indeed, traces of Hera's value to Ancient Greek worship can be seen through some of the oldest and largest ruins strewn about the Mediterranean; of all the temples still standing, Hera's are the most impressive. Though she had a large presence in her husband's patron city, Olympia, Hera's primary temple was located on the island of Samos, far to the east of mainland Greece, the ruins of which still stand to this day. Herodotus described it as "the largest temple we know of," and one can imagine that to be the case merely by looking at what remains. While the temple rose far from the bulk of Greece, it remained an important part of Greek religious culture as the mythological place of Hera's birth.

Myths

We see that the most common trait associated with Hera through her myths is jealousy. It is easy to dismiss her reactions against Zeus, his mortal lovers, and illegitimate children on these grounds alone, but we must keep in mind that Hera above all, as a deity symbolizing marriage and family, is a representation of stability. When such structure as the family and marriage becomes threatened, or as in poor Hera's many cases, violated, the natural reaction is revenge, particularly for the divine-minded, as we have seen in previous generations.

One interesting disparity we see between the king and queen of Olympus comes in the form of transformation, no pun intended. While Zeus has the impulse and ability to transform himself into any creature he wishes, Hera's abilities are inverse; her strengths lie in transforming others into what she wishes. One reason for this could be that as a goddess, Hera's form must necessarily be perfect or ideal; she cannot become anything less than befits her. We see this manifest many times in Greek mythology: Hera turns her wrath outward, cursing and destroying the lives of those who interfere with her marriage. Take, for instance, the myth of the nymph Echo. In one of his many marital transgressions, Zeus insists on covering his tracks by recruiting Echo to occupy Hera by talking incessantly. The conversation sours, of course, when Hera learns of its true purpose and subsequently curses Echo; for all eternity, the nymph will be doomed to lend her voice only to mimicking the voices and words of others.

We see Hera protecting her house and crown once more in the myth of Io, another of Zeus' mortal lovers. To protect Io from the wrath of his wife, Zeus had her transformed into a cow, though Hera, wise and clever as she was, begged Zeus to give her the cow as a present. What strikes the reader is that throughout these myths involving Hera, though Zeus seems to run rampant and with unchecked authority throughout the mortal world, he can never deny his queen. As such, he forfeits the cow, Io, to his wife, who locks her up with golden chains and sets the hundred-eyed Argus to guard her around the clock. Argus, with all his eyes, only closed fifty at any given time, and thus was an excellent watchman. The story holds that Zeus, overcome with a desire to see Io, recruits Hermes to distract, or by some accounts, kill Argus and set Io free. In one account, Hermes does so by lulling all one hundred eyes to sleep with pan pipes, in other accounts, by blinding and killing the hundred-eyed watchman, but nonetheless freeing the white heifer Io. Hera, in response, sent a gadfly to the earth to perpetually sting Io for all eternity, never allowing her to rest, and so, Io wanders the earth forever.

What is striking is that for all the vengeance Hera takes upon her husband's consorts, for all the jealousy she feels, she never once exacts her revenge upon her husband. Perhaps this is because it would violate one of her tenets: that her intent is always to tend toward stability and security within the family circle; undermining or overthrowing the king of the gods, we can easily imagine, would certainly go well against that.

Poseidon

The third major Olympian we have already briefly mentioned in one of Zeus' stories: Poseidon, the lord of the depths of the ocean, master of horses and storms. In his representations, we see him most often proudly striding forward, his telltale trident held aloft. From this trident's forks, springs would erupt from the earth, and rivers would carve their way through the land. His other symbols include a horse, a dolphin, and a fish.

In addition to his mastery of the watery world, he also garners the title "Earth Shaker" in several Greek stories, and as such, has additionally been known as the harbinger of earthquakes. Perhaps he owes this honor to his association with horses, as herds of the creatures have been known to shake the earth as they move. The Ancient Greeks also presumed that the phenomenon of the earthquake was the result of water eroding the rocks of the earth, which also contributes to Poseidon's title. In his role as king of the sea, Poseidon is also responsible for the well-being of sailors and seafarers, though, as we will see in some of his stories, he can be anything but benevolent.

Given that much of Ancient Greece's territories were chains of islands and its people unrivaled sailors, it is no small surprise that Poseidon featured prominently as the principal deity in more cities than Zeus. While he had a prominent presence in Olympia, as with his brother and sister, Poseidon boasted magnificent temples in Corinth, Magna Graecia in southern Italy, and even vied for dominance with Athena for the city of her namesake, Athens.

Poseidon fathered many children with many lovers, not all of them human. From him, we get the winged horse Pegasus, the Cyclopes Polyphemus, the hero and king Theseus, and Orion the hunter, to name only a prodigious few. We see again the prominence Poseidon held in Greek culture; as he was so prolific in reproduction, it could be argued the Greeks understood the value of water as a direct correlation between life and death. Of all the Olympians, Poseidon, possibly due to the proximity of his domain, is the most often tempted to violate the divine agreement regarding the earth's self-governance. In many of his stories, we see his desire to take revenge on the mortal world for trespasses committed against him or his children.

Myths

One of the most iconic myths surrounding Poseidon lies in Homer's Odyssey. In the legendary Trojan War, Poseidon had chosen the side of the ultimately victorious Greeks against the Trojans. On Odysseus' seafaring journey back home, he crosses paths with Polyphemus, who we know is Poseidon's son, and ultimately blinds him, which invokes the unbridled rage of the sea god. Poseidon begs his brother and sister to allow him to punish the transgression of the mortal Odysseus, a request which is denied. Poseidon, Zeus, and Hera agree to a compromise, however. Poseidon may delay Odysseus' journey home, punish those around him, but must not harm Odysseus himself. As a result, we are given the Odyssey, a magnificent work of man's struggle against himself and the world, a story positively worth reading, and within which Poseidon's behaviors and actions are expounded upon in astounding detail.

As hinted earlier, Poseidon was in direct competition with Athena for the city of her namesake, wherein priests and priestesses of both cults maintained an extremely healthy presence. The myth states that on a mutually agreed upon feast date, to decide the patron deity of the city, both cultic processions would set up altars to their respective deities. Seeing this, Poseidon and Athena agreed to each give a gift to the city and let the people decide which divine should hold court in the principal temple. Athena bestowed upon the people of Athens an olive tree, a gift that provided wood, food, shade, and beauty to the Athenians. Poseidon, for his part, struck the ground with his trident and caused a spring to rush forth from the earth; the water, however, was ocean water, salty and briny and entirely unfit for a use other than sailing. Naturally, the Athenians chose Athena's practical and graceful gift, and a furious, rejected Poseidon, his pride wounded, struck the earth once more with such force and rage that he flooded the entire Attic plain to punish the Athenians. The flood reached all the way to the halls of the Erechtheion, an all-marble temple atop the Athenian acropolis devoted to both Athena and Poseidon, which still stands to this day. From the north porch of the temple, the only place in Athens not to be affected by the mythical flood, one can see in the distance where Poseidon allegedly struck his trident: rocky pools known as the "salt sea."

We see that Poseidon is just as vengeful, violent, and jealous as his two siblings, although, as evidenced by his stories, his wrath manifests in a unique way. Both his brother and sister, the king and queen of the Olympians, tend to exercise their power by transforming and dominating individuals, altering physical forms of themselves and others to attain their desired result, coercing them through trickery and deceit. Poseidon, on the other hand, has no such ability; he, as the "Earth Shaker," prefers to unleash his retribution through sheer, natural force. He has no qualm with laying waste to entire peoples for the transgressions of one person. He, unlike any other

Olympian, manipulates with unrelenting savagery the weather and natural world, which, coupled with his notoriously short fuse and protective, paternal instinct, make him arguably the single most feared and revered deity in the entire Ancient Greek pantheon.

Chapter 4:

Girl Power

We move now from our most prominent three deities to three somewhat less visible, but no less powerful goddesses: Athena, who we mentioned briefly in our quarrel with Poseidon, the goddess of wisdom, Artemis, the chaste, untamable huntress, and Aphrodite, the most sensual and passionate of all the divines. We are placing these three in the same chapter not based on any generational or genealogical lines but because they occupy distinctly feminine places in Ancient Greek culture, and as we will see, oftentimes, these places are infinitely more powerful and influential than the male-dominated, location-based domains.

We can argue that the trifecta of female deities hold much more power because their domains are primarily internal: they are the heart and mind, which yield the cosmic magic of emotion and language, which dominates the world of mortals and permeates the realm of the divines. We will see that for all their infallibility and rage, their jealousy and omnipotence, even the fiercest and mightiest Olympians must succumb at some point to the eternally dominant intangibles of love and logic.

Athena

By this point, we have become briefly introduced to Athena; we know her patron city, and we know how it came into her possession. She was the goddess of wisdom, warfare and its strategy, and handicraft, three things that her namesake of Athens excelled at in the ancient world. She is often depicted in a traditional Greek warrior's helmet and holding a spear, and is one of, if not the only, Greek goddess who is depicted exclusively fully clothed. From her gift to the Athenians, we can gather that one of her symbols is the olive and its tree, symbols of Greek prosperity, and she also claims the owl as her bird, the snake as her animal, and a pendant depicting the head of a Gorgon, called the *Gorgoneion*.

Of all the Greek pantheon, no deity is so quick to aid a righteous mortal than Athena. Throughout her stories, she incessantly appears in various disguises to support a hero or thwart a malevolent divine hand. She, according to myth, aided nearly every single prominent Greek hero: Jason, Heracles, Perseus, and Bellerophon, among others. She is the guiding light for mortal man through the darkness of the unknown, and thus it is no surprise that her image in the Western world of art has become synonymous with democratic principles and the idea of freedom. According to Plato, Athena's name can be broken down to mean "divine intelligence," which, given her myths of guiding heroes toward their goals and belaying ill-intended plans of the gods, gives her an air that floats toward the concept of "fate;" she operates in spite of and above the divine level of her siblings.

Myths

Athena, by all accounts, is said to have been birthed by unique circumstances. She was the child of Zeus and Metis, one of Zeus's early wives. According to a prophecy, as are so common in the ancient world, it was said that Metis would birth two children more powerful than Zeus himself: a son and a daughter, who, of course, would ultimately overthrow Zeus. Following in his own father's footsteps, Zeus turned his pregnant wife into a fly and swallowed her before she could give birth to the children. Within Zeus's stomach, to protect her first child, she began forging Athena's iconic Grecian helmet and her ever-present robe, understanding that in time her child would be born. The constant hammering of the helmet's construction gave Zeus an immense headache, and he demanded Hephaestus, or by some accounts, Prometheus, obtain a double-headed ax and split his head in two. From the wound, Athena sprang forth, fully grown and donning her helmet. Because she emerged from the head of Zeus, she is given her domain of divine intelligence and is often regarded as Zeus' favorite child.

What is interesting is that she uses this divine intelligence not to control the realm of the divines, but rather, as we have mentioned, aid in the accomplishing of mortal tasks. Countless images of Athena have been collected portraying her alongside Heracles, and several poetic sources show her lending a hand to the nearly defeated hero. She is given reign over the hearts and minds of humanity in a way unique from all other divines; undoubtedly, being the favorite child of the king of the gods comes with certain privileges, and perhaps more than one blind eye. What we see manifest in her "divine intelligence" is lending her power to those who prefer cunning and strategy over those who rush headlong into any combat.

For example, we see in Homer's Odyssey, one instance in which Athena favors those mortals gifted with wit. Odysseus, who is a master of cunning and a highly intelligent and practical combatant, becomes a protégé of and thus protected by Athena. She reveals herself to him on many occasions and speaks on his behalf atop Mount Olympus, pleading to her father to let Odysseus return home after his ten years at sea. She speaks to his friends and relatives, bringing discoveries and news of Odysseus' whereabouts and condition to their attention. Odysseus, meanwhile, has fallen into countless traps and captures, all through his human folly, though with his intelligence and practical thinking, emerges relatively unscathed, though the same cannot be said of his compatriots. We are treated to an Ancient Greek version of "creating one's own luck;" it is due to the similar, intellectually creative natures of Odysseus and Athena that bring them together.

Though Athena appears to meddle benevolently in the affairs of mankind, being a divine and a direct offspring of Zeus, she is not without her wrathful side. There are many myths featuring a side of wise Athena that is just as jealous and vengeful as her father. One of the more interesting stories to emerge is the tale of the Gorgon Medusa. Medusa was a priestess in one of Athena's many temples and was, according to myth, exceptionally beautiful. Poseidon, with his insatiable appetite, lusted after the priestess, disregarding the vow of chastity she had taken, and seduced her on the floor of Athena's temple. Once she had learned of this desecration, Athena turned the beautiful Medusa into the snake-haired monster we imagine today, with a gaze that would turn any mortal into stone.

Artemis

Our second powerful female deity comes in the form of the elusive and cunning Artemis. The goddess of the hunt, Artemis, is often shown brandishing a bow and quiver, which are symbols of her efficacy in the wilds. Alongside her, most commonly, are deer, her sacred animal, and like her counterpart Athena, she too claims a tree as a divine symbol: the cypress. She is the divine huntress, the goddess of the wilderness, protector of young women, and guardian of the moon; indeed, above all other deities in the Greek pantheon, not a single one is more ethereal, and not a single one is more graceful. In the true fashion of the divine huntress, myths and stories of her exploits are difficult to track down; not many texts regarding her history survive.

Another child of Zeus, she was a twin of Apollo, as the stories go. By some accounts, she is older and even assisted in the birth of Apollo, and by others, the two were born simultaneously. Her mother was Leto, a daughter of the two Titans Phoebe and Coeus. Despite the lack of surviving written work about Artemis, there is a myriad of physical representations that have passed through the centuries; this shows that perhaps while not as important in the codification of religious or cultic mythologies, she could have played an immense part in the daily life and worship of the Greeks. Her domain is adjacent and runs parallel to many of her sisters, as she helps to ensure the survivability of mankind through the prosperity of their hunts and protection of their women. What is interesting about Artemis' personality is that she seems not only to insist upon her chastity for all eternity but also seems to remain a young girl forever, like an Ancient Greek Peter Pan.

As she was one of the most-worshipped deities in the ancient Mediterranean, it stands to reason that her temples would befit that title. Her patron city was Ephesus, in modern day Turkey, wherein a temple was constructed in her name that became one of the Seven Wonders of the Ancient World. Unfortunately, due to centuries of conquest and human negligence, only ruins remain at the site of the once-towering temple. However, its presence reinforces Artemis' divine importance as a goddess in practical, everyday life, as though her existence is a harbor in the storms and divine wrath of the unknown.

Myths

We are told and can most likely deduce, given our experience with the hyperbolic pantheon, that Artemis is a young woman of staggering beauty. She is so beautiful that she catches not only the eye of Zeus and several other male divines but also the eye of Hera. Hera, however, is extremely jealous of Artemis' beauty and the attention lavished upon her by her male counterparts, and as is her way, cursed her to remain in the form of a young girl. In Homer's *Iliad*, we are treated to a glimpse of Artemis after her transformation, as she is represented as a crying child upon the lap of Zeus, and in a poem by Callimachus, the weeping child Artemis is granted ten wishes by her father, which effectively establish her domain. Among her ten wishes, she asks for: any city, which we know to be Ephesus, to remain chaste forever, a bow and arrow forged by the Cyclopes, a choir of nymphs comprised Oceanus' daughters, and a knee-length tunic so that she may not be impeded while hunting. She also asked for the ability to relieve the pains of childbirth, as she had witnessed them firsthand with the birth of her brother Apollo.

Another myth surrounding the elusive Artemis involves the protection of her chastity, a recurring theme throughout the surviving stories about her. In this instance, during a hunt, Artemis stops to rest and bathe in a stream. Through the woods comes Actaeon, an extremely skillful hunter in his own right, nearly as quiet and observant as Artemis herself. He chances upon the goddess bathing, which means he has seen her in the nude and is caught in the act by Artemis herself. To punish him for watching her, she turns the hunter into a stag, who is then viciously and mercilessly hunted down by his own pack of hunting dogs who cannot distinguish the animal from their master.

Though Artemis was pursued by many male suitors, only one man ever won her heart: the great, giant hunter named Orion, one of the many sons of Poseidon. Myth states that Artemis and Orion were hunting partners, and he charmed her through his skill with a bow. He boasted that he could successfully hunt any creature upon the earth and threatened in his time with Artemis to kill them all. Gaia, the earth mother, having heard this, became determined to create a creature whose skin could not only withstand the arrows of Orion's bow but also equal the hunter's lethal talent with a dagger. Thus, the scorpion was born. According to one version of the myth, Artemis' brother Apollo conspired with Gaia to create the scorpion to destroy Orion, as he disapproved of his sister's cavorting with a male and was overprotective of her maidenhood. By some accounts, during the ensuing combat between the two hunters and the scorpion, Artemis mistakenly shot and killed Orion with her own divine bow and arrow; in her grief, she immortalized Orion as the constellation we see today.

Aphrodite

Born of the waves and erogenous zones of the first Father Time, Aphrodite is by far the most seductive and irresistible goddess in the entire pantheon. Hers is the realm of love, passion, the erotic, and physical beauty. No other deity in any other pantheon comes close to Aphrodite's charm and sensual persuasiveness; even certain foods have come to carry her namesake for their purported qualities. "Aphrodisiacs" are said to accelerate sexual appetite and desire, which fall almost too perfectly in the basket of our goddess of love.

Her symbols have survived the centuries, maintaining their erotic and passionate connotations: the pearl, the scallop shell, the rose, and mirror, all have attributes that orbit the world of carnal passion and sensual delight. Her animals were the dove and tortoise, and some sources indicate her affinity for the dolphin as well. We know she emerged from a union between the sea and Uranus' severed genitals; the mythological location of that union is, according to the poet Sappho, the bay of Paphos on the island of Cyprus. Others place her birth off the island of Crete, along a major sea trade route for the Greeks. Wherever her birthplace, we know that by all accounts, she was born a fully grown adult with no childhood, skilled in the ways of passion, and a highly desirable woman. Among her many epithets, one of the most telling of her domain is Aphrodite, the "Genital-Lover." Given her domain of the purely sexual, one can easily imagine that she is often portrayed in the nude, or when she is clothed, the fabric seems to be mere drapery, concealing little of her assuredly feminine figure. She and her niece Athena are the only two Olympians to have been born immaculately: Athena from the head of Zeus, and Aphrodite from the sea.

Aphrodite, for all her appeal, was widely worshipped across the ancient Mediterranean, from Athens to her birthplace Cyprus, and even as far south as Alexandria in Egypt. She had major temples and sites of worship all throughout Greece, and every year in Athens, a celebration would be held in her honor: the Aphrodisia. During this festival, priests would sacrifice a dove to Aphrodite in gratitude for her role in uniting Greece. She has been the inspiration and basis for countless works of art, ranging from paintings to sculptures and character archetypes in novels, plays, and stories, and continues in many regards to represent a certain form of ideal sensuality.

Myths

One theme that emerges from Aphrodite's mythological history is that her beauty and amorous nature tend to get other people in trouble. It also ignites repeatedly the all too quick tempers of the fickle Olympians, particularly her sisters and nieces, who, in turn, insist on punishing the unsuspecting mortal population. Unlike her siblings, though, Aphrodite never seems to care about the consequences of her actions; she is the manifestation of moments of passion, not the guilt or regret that follows.

Take, for example, her feud with Hera and Athena, two major players in the Greek religious world. All three claimed ownership of a golden apple cast to the earth by Eris, the goddess of discord, which held the inscription "to the fairest." Naturally, all three goddesses thought themselves the fairest, and took their case before Zeus. Unable, or perhaps unwilling, to decide himself, Zeus handed the decision to a mortal prince: Paris of Troy. As all divine beauty is unparalleled to mortal eyes, Paris could not decide, and the three resorted to bribery. Athena promised Paris fame and glory in battle, Hera offered him control of the continents Asia and Europe, but Aphrodite, with her unique power over the hearts and parts of man, confided in Paris that if he should choose her, he would be able to marry the most beautiful woman in the world. Naturally, given his mortal weaknesses, Paris chose Aphrodite and was gifted his prize: Helen, daughter of King Menelaus of Sparta. Paris' decision enraged Hera and Athena, who broke from Mount Olympus and instigated the legendary Trojan War on the side of the Spartans. Aphrodite, fitting her personality of momentary passion, was content with her apple and title, and never rushed into battle herself, though she did find her way into several heroes' bedrooms.

Aphrodite, to a degree far surpassing her Olympian counterparts, favors mortals whom she finds physically attractive, while giving no real preference for the divines. While it is true that she is technically married, this is not by her choice, as we will see later when we dive into the stories of Hephaestus. She seems obsessed with manipulating the hearts of men, particularly those who devote their worship entirely to her. In that way, she can certainly be the most selfish of the Olympians, even though her actions, for the most part, seem flippant and impulsive. One prominent instance of this is in the myth of Pygmalion. Pygmalion was a brilliant sculptor who could carve the most magnificent figures from marble. He was convinced that all women were immoral and essentially evil, so he refused to marry or keep the company of any female. However, he was a devout worshipper of Aphrodite, even going so far as to carve her likeness out of stone. During the artistic process, Pygmalion fell in love with the statue and longed to marry it. Aphrodite, impressed by his devotion to her, granted life to the statue and thus Pygmalion's wishes.

To Conclude

We see that these goddesses are equally terrifying and beautiful in their power. They occupy the spaces of mortal minds, bodies, and hearts, although not in the purely physical way. Each of their strengths comes from indirectly controlling and guiding those internal impulses that lead us away from the purely animal and toward the distinctly human. The powers of wit, the hunt, and procreation are three of the most essential elements of survival in the ancient world for mankind. Entrusting those necessary pieces to three of the most widely-worshipped deities in the pantheon illustrates in a small way the importance of the female presence in Ancient Greece, and with what quiet respect it was regarded.

Chapter 5:

Let's Hear It for the Boys

A truth of the universe is that everything must ultimately come into balance; the Greek pantheon is no exception. For the subtle powers in the realm of the psyche bestowed upon the earth by the three major female deities, there must be brothers who reign from Mount Olympus with heavier, more blatant hands. This brings us to our next triad of male deities in the subsequent generation of Olympians: Apollo the miracle worker, the raging and violent Ares, and the swift Hermes.

This trio is grouped as such as they bear genealogical resemblance to the previous three goddesses; Apollo, we know, is Artemis' sister, Ares, a lover of Aphrodite, and Hermes, a favorite son of Zeus. We will see that their realms are more concrete than their female counterparts, although they seem to share conceptual lifting; it could be said that they and their sisters are two sides of the same coin. We will see that all three are, without a doubt, sons of their father Zeus, as in some capacity, they all carry a specific trait of his character.

Apollo

The younger twin of Artemis, Apollo, shares many of her qualities. His weapon is the bow and arrow, just as is Artemis', though he claims the swan as his bird, and the python as his animal. While his sister is the protector of young women, Apollo is charged with the protection of young men, and, as such, he is the principal figure of the ancient Greek nation. A distinction should be made: it could be said that Zeus is the principal representative of the Greeks, but he is specifically chief of the gods, religiously speaking. That is, he is the surviving religious artifact that the Greeks gave to the Western world; when it comes to national and international affairs, it is Apollo who is the representation of Ancient Greece's cities and people. He is seen as a deity of healing and, specifically, medicine; his python, along with his son, Asclepius, intertwine around that eponymous symbol of Western medicine, the Rod of Asclepius.

In addition to his role as a healer, Apollo was music and art made manifest; he is often depicted in the company of the Muses, strumming his lyre. Initially, in the Greek tradition, he was a deity rurally inclined; he looked over shepherds and their flocks, presumably in his role as protector of the young. Later, as Greek civilization grew to become more urban and less nomadic, he was the ever-watchful patron over the blossoming democracy and the founding of new Greek cities. Given his importance and rise to prominence along with Greek civilization, he is deemed by several sources as an amalgam of all gods; in essence, he is the perfect eternal youth, brimming with potential.

Though he had temples devoted to his many faces throughout the ancient Mediterranean, his most important place of worship was at Delphi, the fabled site of the legendary oracle. This site housed that eponymous oracle, who, in fact, was a worshipper of Apollo and was traditionally a young woman. Unlike other deities and their followers, Apollo's worshippers touted the strongest connection with the oracular and clairvoyant; should any person of note wish to discover their fate, they would ultimately head for Delphi in hopes of obtaining the blessing of the keeper of Greek civilization.

Myths

Leto, one of Zeus' many wives, gave birth to her children on the floating land of Delos, as Zeus had forbidden her to give birth on earth. First, she gave birth to Artemis, who acted as a midwife for the delivery of her brother, Apollo. When Apollo emerged, he held a golden sword, and the story says that everything on Delos then turned into gold. Swans were said to have circled the island. He was fed ambrosia and clothed in fine, white cloth held in place with golden bands. After having eaten the nectar of the gods, the child Apollo tore the bands from his body, announcing that he alone would be the interpreter of Zeus' will to mankind. Allegedly, it was the god's birth that anchored

Delos to the earth and rendered it an important place of Apollo worship throughout Ancient Grecian history.

Apollo, according to myth, was responsible for slaying Python, the enormous snake, the midwife of the giant Typhon, and supplicant of Hera. As per Hera's orders, Python attempts to assassinate the pregnant Leto to prevent the birth of Artemis and Apollo. Python, while successful in harassing and assaulting Leto, failed to kill her. After his birth, the child Apollo vowed revenge, and picking up his bow and arrow, hunted Python down and killed it in the very cave at Delphi that would bear his temple and oracle.

While Apollo was known chiefly as a healer and protector, he could also be known to dispense suffering and death. Several accounts show him as a plague-bringer, particularly during times of hardship. During the Trojan War, for example, when, on the side of Troy in defense of that city, he sent a terrible plague upon the invading Greek camp. During that conflict, he was responsible for the destruction of many Greek heroes, Achilles included.

The laurel wreath as a symbol of triumph stemmed from Apollo as well. Myth states that Apollo, having been struck with Cupid's fabled arrow, fell in love with Daphne, a forest nymph. As a chaste devotee of the woods, Daphne scorned Apollo's advances, who, in turn, took to pursuing her through the forest to try and change her mind. Daphne, whose cries for help Gaia heard, was transformed into a laurel tree. In some stories, Gaia hides Daphne deep within the forest and replaces her with the laurel tree, but the fact remains: Apollo loved the tree and donned its leaves and branches as a symbol of his victory. Even today, we see the connotation of Ancient Greek culture and the laurel leaf; it seems that when the iconography of Ancient Greece emerges, one of the first images to appear is the laurel wreath.

Ares

Just like his sister Athena, Ares is a manifestation of warfare. Unlike his sister, who centers herself on the tactics, planning, and leadership of war, he is the image of and delights in the horrors of combat; his is the realm of brutality, carnage, and indiscriminate slaughter. While Athena is pictured with her iconic helmet and robes, Ares is often depicted entirely nude, sporting a similar helmet, and wielding a shield. Among his symbols, he counts his shield, spear, chariot, and flaming torch; his animal companions consist of the boar, the dog, and that most vile of all avian beings: the vulture.

Though a decidedly warlike people, the Ancient Greeks surprisingly held little regard for Ares as a powerful, prominent deity. There appears to be a differentiation in Greek thinking between the necessity of war and the senseless destruction it causes; in no means do they elevate that carnage above its status as a "necessary evil." Ares' influence in the world of man as well as atop Mount Olympus is significantly diminished when compared to his sister's; Zeus himself tells his son in one story that he, in Zeus' eyes, is the most despised of all gods. In Sparta, however, Ares was elevated beyond his role as the harbinger of pain, death, and destruction and became associated with the ideal soldier, though this image is widely regarded as different than the majority of Greece.

Ares had few temples devoted to him in the ancient world, unlike his Roman counterpart Mars, who was a pivotal deity in that culture's pantheon. It could even be argued that due to his maligned place among the Olympians, that Ares was not Greek at all; indeed, myths point to Thrace as his birthplace, in modern day Turkey, which housed a people the Greeks thought entirely barbaric. We know, however, that as an outlier, Sparta housed a temple devoted to Ares, as well as an enormous statue of the deity in chains outside the city, according to Pausanias.

Upon his chariot, Ares rides into the maelstrom of battle with two of his sons by Aphrodite: Deimos and Phobos, "dread" and "fear," respectively. Decimating the ranks of both sides in battle, Ares chooses no favorites but insists upon rewarding courageous acts and valor in combat. His is a role as indifferent toward the fate of the Greeks as the Greeks are to him; he cares for nothing other than the clash of swords and the falling of bodies around him.

Myths

One of the most widely depicted myths involving Ares is his legendary fight with Heracles. It has been emblazoned on countless numbers of ancient pottery and repeatedly rendered in pigment by classical painters. The story goes that one of Ares' sons, Cygnus, a powerful Thessalian king, would detain travelers and pilgrims on their way to the Oracle at Delphi. In his cruelty, he would treat the travelers to food and drink, and then kill them without compunction. Naturally, this aroused the fury of Apollo, who dispatched Heracles to take revenge on Cygnus. In Apollodorus' Bibliotheca, he writes that the two met in single combat, and with Athena's intervention, Heracles thrust his spear through Cygnus' neck, killing him. Ares, furious not only with his son's murder but with his sister's intervention on behalf of Heracles, rushes to earth to confront Heracles. The two belligerents meet in battle, and again with Athena's aid, Heracles manages to inflict a wound on Ares' thigh. A thunderbolt from Zeus ends the fight, and Ares' two sons, Deimos and Phobos, carry the god of war away from battle and back to Mount Olympus to heal. Other stories recount similar events, though instead of Cygnus' murder by Heracles, he is simply turned into a swan, Apollo's bird, as penance, and became the eponymous constellation we see today.

Another popular myth involving the god of war comes in the form of his conflict with the Aloadae: Otus and Ephialtes, two giants and sons of Poseidon. According to myth, the two giants were responsible for bestowing civilization upon mankind; they grew, according to the writer Hyginus, "nine fingers every month," and were "surpassed in beauty only by Orion." Literally translated, the pair's names are "insatiate" or "insatiable," and "nightmare." They plotted to overthrow the gods atop Mount Olympus by constructing mountains to rival Olympus and claiming Hera and Artemis as their wives. In their war with the Olympians, they managed to capture hotheaded Ares and hold him captive with chains in a bronze jar for thirteen months; the whole time, Ares was screaming and raging for his freedom. However, Eriboea, the mother of the two giants, made the mistake of relating to Hermes her sons' conquest, who, with Artemis' help, freed the captured god of war. Artemis then tricked the giants into impaling each other with their spears by turning into a deer and jumping between them.

What we see time and time again in the myths of Ares is his rashness and headstrong mentality often lands himself in danger or at the mercy of those he strives to fight against. He is often outwitted and outclassed, relying solely on his ability to unleash havoc with brute force upon the earth; it is no surprise then, that for all the fear and terror he strikes into the hearts of the Ancient Greeks, he is easily dispatched and diluted through the workings of other, more "diplomatic" deities.

Hermes

The third wily son of Zeus is Hermes, the young herald, and messenger of Mount Olympus. Renowned for his cleverness and fleetness of foot, he was the ever-alert guardian and protector of the roads, merchants, and traders of the ancient Mediterranean. He also was known as a trickster, and thus became a patron deity of thieves. From him, we have the image of the winged sandals, and among his other symbols are the airy lyre, the crowing rooster, and his winged helmet, known as a Petasos. His tree is the palm, and in his representations, a goat or lamb is usually found somewhere nearby.

His iconography is one of the most interesting of all the Olympians; in early images such as gravestones and stone fragments, he is depicted as a fully grown and bearded adult, his hair curling proudly around his ears and forehead. Later, in Hellenic Greece and even into Roman times, he is shown most often as a child, closer to the Hermes we recognize; he tends to be nude save for his winged sandals, cape, and helmet, clutching his staff of two intertwined serpents.

In addition to his position as guardian of transportation and commerce, Hermes also played the part of divine guide; it was he who helped recently deceased souls into the afterlife. He has also been recognized as the mediator between the visible and invisible worlds. That is, in his role as divine messenger, it is his duty to make the will of Zeus manifest in the material world, while it is his brother Apollo who interprets it. Pieces of evidence of Hermes' places of worship are scant in the ancient world, although there is some reason to believe that he was primarily worshipped extremely devoutly in rural areas of Greece, primarily as a guardian of flocks, shepherds, and farmers. Only three ruins of his temples remain today; all three of these ruins are within the northeastern portion Arcadia, the southern, three-fingered "hand" of mainland Greece. The lack of temples in Hermes' honor might be because his spaces of worship were the roads of Ancient Greece itself; markers bearing Hermes' image have been discovered all along supposed Grecian highways.

While a notorious trickster and confounder of mortals and divines alike, Hermes, according to Pausanias, was dubbed by Zeus to remain entirely amoral. Zeus, according to Homer's hymn to Hermes, decrees that Hermes alone "should be the appointed messenger to Hades, who, though he takes no gift, shall give him no mean prize." Interestingly, his presence in Greek households was supposed to ensure good luck, as Hermes was a "gift giver" and one who bestowed blessings. There is even evidence that in his early cultic years, he was a deity of prosperity and fertility, which we can imagine, for one as agile and swift as Hermes, is not so great a leap. As Ancient Greece became more connected beyond the family circle, who better to look after its prosperity and connections than the deity responsible for creating them?

Myths

We are treated to Hermes' tricks nearly from the moment of his birth. One myth surrounding him states that when he was merely hours old, he snuck from his crib and made off with several of Apollo's divine cattle, hiding them away in a cave in Pylos, along the southwestern coast of Greece. To disguise his footsteps, he first donned his now famous sandals, thus making his feet unidentifiable. Thinking he had gotten away with his theft, he slaughtered several of the oxen in gratitude, performing what the Ancient Greeks agreed was the first animal sacrifice. He then took muscle fiber from one of the sacrificed animals and strung it across a tortoise shell, thus creating the lyre. Apollo, noticing several of his prize cattle missing, tracked them down to Hermes' cave, where Hermes denied ever having seen them. Apollo appealed to his father, Zeus, who, having seen everything, demanded the oxen be returned to Apollo. However, upon hearing the strum of the lyre, Apollo grew infatuated with its music and offered a suitable trade for all parties: the remainder of his herd for Hermes' newly invented instrument. Apollodorus writes to conclude the myth that Zeus was so amused by his young son's gumption that he immediately made him an immortal Olympian.

In addition to helping Zeus free his lover Io and liberating Ares from his bronze jar, Hermes was no stranger to aiding mortals in times of overwhelming crisis. It is shown across many surviving stories and works of ancient art how the messenger god bestowed upon Perseus the necessary equipment to dispatch Medusa. Loaning Perseus his winged sandals, cape, and golden sword, Hermes instructed the hero Perseus in their use: the winged sandals so as to not be heard by the monster, the cape so as to not be seen, and the sword for severing Medusa's head.

In Homer's Odyssey, Hermes appears before a wandering Odysseus with words of warning, in effect, comically chastising him. He tells Odysseus it is dangerous to wander, as the magic-wielding temptress Circe lives on the island, who will undoubtedly try to bewitch the hero with a strong, enchanted drink. Hermes offers Odysseus an herb, telling him to eat it, as it will dispel any harmful effects Circe could place upon him. Odysseus does as the messenger commands, and sure enough, the magic of Circe fails in turning the hero into a pig, saving him from the fate of many of his shipmates.

We can see Hermes draws some distinct comparisons between himself and Athena, our wisest, most measured Olympian. Both deities see the value in assisting humans with their advancement; indeed, it could be argued that it is part of their job descriptions. Athena, due to her wisdom, was often equated with education and, specifically, human growth through technology; the advent of farm equipment, for example, is a gift from the goddess. Hermes occupies a similar space, although his methods of aiding human development come from trade, commerce, and intercommunication between peoples; his gifts to mankind include the alphabet, currency, and the wheel.

To Conclude

Between the three looming male figures and the previously exalted female deities, we can decipher striking similarities; beyond the familial relationships, many of these six gods share the roles of their siblings. As we have stated, these pairs of deities are essentially two sides of the same coin, adhering to more or less "traditional" behavior patterns; the male counterparts tend toward the side of the boastful, rash, and aggressive in their interactions with the world. This does not necessarily mean they occupy an "evil" side of Greek religious thought; as has been stated previously, it is impossible to brand any of these stories or figures with a moral tag. They are figurative representations of ill-understood concepts, offering, despite the terror they inspire or gifts they bestow, a working model for the people of Ancient Greece.

Chapter 6:

Last But Not Least

While we seem to have the most prominent of the Greek pantheon covered, surely there must be parts of the world, both divine and mortal, left undefined. We have seen that many of the roles of the most famous deities intersect and overlap, but between them all, they certainly must have let some parts of the world slip through their widely-cast net. What of the crops that sprout from the furrows of Athena's plow? What of the revelry reaped from a good harvest? What of the home behind the grain that holds the revelry? And what of the steel that crafts the plow, and those who craft the steel? Are not all these just as, if not more important to humanity than wisdom, war, or water?

These questions bring us to our final four Olympians: Hephaestus, Demeter, Dionysus, and Hestia. While they dwell mostly in the shadow of their boisterous and interloping brothers and sisters, the four are an essential part of Ancient Greek life and culture. They, above all, represent the peace and security that civilization and family can provide. While their brothers and sisters are the pillars of Greek religion, hoisting the divine shelter above the Greek people's heads, our remaining deities can be seen as the four corners of the temple foundation upon which those pillars stand, holding them unshakably firm and tall through the centuries.

Hephaestus

The lord of craftsmanship, its tools and metal itself, Hephaestus' work is renowned across Greece and throughout the pantheon. He claims the anvil, tongs, and hammer as his tool, and from beneath Mount Olympus, he alone is responsible for controlling the fires of the earth. Due to his exemplary, almost miraculous metalwork, he is the patron of sculptors and artists alike and the ever-watchful friend of the carpenter. He is known to look after the work of blacksmiths, going so far as to infuse his own metalwork into that of chosen mortal workers.

To the Ancient Greeks, Hephaestus occupied an important, if oftentimes uncelebrated, role as the master of industry and artisan craftsmanship. His presence could be noticed, fittingly, in the urban city centers of the Ancient Greek world; these were, of course, the primary locations of workshops and armories. According to Homer's Iliad, the island of Lemnos was Hephaestus' home when he struck out from Olympus. Today, evidence of cultic activity can be seen strewn about the north Aegean island's ruins, and in particular, through the distinct, exceptional quality of the ancient tools unearthed there.

A son of Hera, he was cast from the top of Mount Olympus and his seat with the divines for a deformed or misshapen foot. He is the only deity in the Greek pantheon to have a noted physical deviation; all the other divines are repeatedly lavished with the praise of perfection and represented as ideal forms. As he could not be physically perfect himself, he devoted his divine talents to crafting physically perfect objects: swords, armor, even Hermes' winged sandals. Among his companions and assistants, he counted the Cyclopes, the very three who forged Zeus' thunderbolt, as well as automatons composed of metal.

Hephaestus' iconography, just like his deformity, is unique to the Greek pantheon as well. As he possessed unrivaled skill in metal and stone, it was written of Hephaestus that he could bring life to any inanimate object; we see one instance of this in his workshop automatons. What this meant for his iconography was that it became imbued with the god's presence; the images rendered of Hephaestus in stone or metal, on a tombstone or edifice, were not mere representations of the god, but a literal manifestation of the god himself. Given the awe-inspiring artistic and architectural works produced by the Ancient Greeks and their influence on the Western world, it is easy to see how, even back then, the Greeks found the beauty of craftsmanship divine.

Myths

Hephaestus, the master craftsman that he is, was recruited by Zeus to construct all the thrones in the Palace of Olympus. This, of course, was after his casting off the mountain by his mother, Hera. Hephaestus did as he was told, building the immaculate seats for his eleven relatives. Upon sitting on her throne, Hera found that it began to levitate, and suspended her between the realms of heaven and earth. When she demanded that her son and throne's builder help her down on matriarchal grounds, Hephaestus replied famously, "I have no mother." To make amends, Hera offered her son any hand in marriage he could desire; Hephaestus chose Aphrodite, the goddess of love.

Some of the most interesting myths surrounding Hephaestus are tied to his marriage. His wife is Aphrodite, the picture of beauty and desire. It seems incongruous that a sulking, lame blacksmith and the queen of sexuality would match, and in a certain sense, one would not be wrong for thinking so. Aphrodite's infidelity is widely touted throughout Greek mythology; her numerous affairs are each of a mythological caliber, even for a deity. One affair in particular catches our eye, just as it caught Hephaestus': her transgression with Ares, the god of war.

We know that Ares, for all his terror and bluster, is irrational, short-sighted, and frankly, none too intelligent. During the Trojan War, he took up a secret relationship with Aphrodite, and due to his carelessness, was caught in the act by Helios as he was driving his chariot of the sun across the sky. Naturally, as the bringer of light, Helios informed Hephaestus of his wife's infidelity to which the blacksmith responded in silence, crafting and drafting plans for revenge. He set to work in his workshop, crafting by some accounts a net, by some accounts chains, but by all accounts bronze and fine as threads of silk, and strong enough to ensnare even the mightiest of gods. He set his trap upon his bed, and sure enough, caught the two lovers. Hephaestus then called down from Olympus all the gods to bear witness and humiliate the two paramours. Seeing the state of the two entangled gods, Poseidon pleads to Hephaestus to release them, vowing that all penalties shall be paid by Ares, and if he should fail, Poseidon himself will take up the shackles of Hephaestus. Satisfied, the divine craftsman releases the two, whereupon a disgraced Ares returns to his distant homeland of Thrace, and Aphrodite to the sea from whence she came, bathing herself to restore her virginity. The punishment alluded to by Poseidon was never paid by Ares directly, though we are told that his children would bear ill-fated destinies.

Given his stature as an artisan, it is no surprise that Zeus entrusts his forging and crafting to no other than Hephaestus. It was the divine sculptor himself who was charged with bringing to form the most beautiful mortal woman known to the world. Tired of the advances of his female counterparts upon the men of the mortal plane, and as a price demanded of mankind for illicitly acquiring fire, Zeus commanded that

Hephaestus bring to life Pandora, which he did from clay and water. Zeus instructed Hephaestus to render, according to Hesiod, her "face like the immortal goddesses, [with] the bewitching features of a young girl." She was to be so fully beautiful, charming, and intelligent that she would be "a sorrow to men who eat bread." In addition to giving form to Pandora, Hephaestus also crafted Pandora's infamous *pithos*, a jar often mistranslated as a "box," from which, opening in her curiosity, she released all evil into the world.

Demeter

For putting food on the table, the Greeks have Demeter to thank. She is the mother of the harvest, a culmination of Gaia and Athena, the giver of growth and grain. In addition to her role as the proverbial founder of the feast, she also holds in her hands the cycle of life and death; she dictates the natural order of things. Genealogically speaking, she is among the newer Olympians, though one can trace her existence in her form as the mother of agriculture further back than almost any Olympian deity.

Demeter's symbols include wheat, the torch, the cornucopia, and bread. Curiously, she does not claim an animal as her living symbol, nor is she often associated with many male lovers. As the manifestation of the bounty of the earth, she is represented alongside or within various flowers and greenery, most specifically the poppy, which thrives in fields of grain throughout the Mediterranean. If not rendered alone, she is often pictured alongside her daughter Persephone, whose absence from the earth via her marriage to Hades brought about the advent of winter.

Demeter boasted one of the largest and most famous cults of the ancient world. Her patron city was Eleusis, along mainland Greece's southeastern coast. Every year, pilgrims would flock to Eleusis to take part in the Eleusinian Mysteries, a festival devoted to the harvest goddess and her daughter Persephone. The festival was ancient even by Grecian standards; elements of it can be traced to the Mycenaean period several hundred years before Homer's epics, and it survived to be adapted by Romans in their worship of Ceres. The Mysteries centered on the myth of Persephone's disappearance into the underworld and her journey back to earth and was divided into ritual parts as such: her descent, the search for her, and her ascent.

The goddess of the harvest also enjoyed the splendor of a universal, localized festival throughout Greece, known as the Thesmophoria. This ritual took place in late October, and according to various sources, restricted its attendance to adult women. This festival was intended to promote fertility and reproduction for women, which may explain its yearly occurrence around the time when the harvest would take place.

Myths

Given the allegorical prominence of Demeter's festivals, it stands to reason that the most important myth surrounding the Grain Mother has to do with Persephone's disappearance into the depths of the underworld. The story is rendered most vividly and coherently by Homer, in his hymn to Demeter. Homer writes that one day in Zeus' fields, Demeter's daughter Persephone and several nymphs of Oceanus were singing and gathering flowers in a Grecian Garden of Eden, which by Gaia were "made to grow at the will of Zeus, and to please Hades, to be a snare for the blossom-like [Persephone]." Hades, seizing his opportunity, mounted his chariot and kidnapped Persephone from her garden, dragging her to the underworld. Persephone cried for help, though all her shouting went unheard by Zeus and his Olympian companions atop the mountain except for her attentive mother.

Having heard her daughter's cries for help, Demeter threw off her cloak and descended Mount Olympus with all haste. She ran over land and sea, searching everywhere for her Persephone. She asked every man and animal she came across what had become of her daughter, though none would answer truthfully, if at all. Homer writes that this pattern of searching continued for nine days. Just before the dawn of the tenth day, Demeter encountered on her travels a torch-wielding Hera, who consequently had been searching for the missing Demeter. The harvest goddess revealed to Hera why she had fled Mount Olympus, that her daughter had vanished amid cries for help, and that it was her motherly duty to rescue her. Remaining silent, Hera took Demeter by the hand, and by the light of her torch, she escorted her to the foot of Helios' chariot.

Helios' responsibility, as we know, is riding the chariot of the sun across the sky every day. He is also the eternal watchman of both realms: the mortal and the divine. As no man or beast would reveal truthfully Persephone's whereabouts, it was left to the forthright Helios to alleviate Demeter's grieving. He informed her that he had seen Persephone whisked away by Hades' chariot to the underworld, where, Hades claimed, he would make a wife of Persephone. As is in his objective nature, however, Helios makes the argument that as far as a husband goes, Persephone could do a lot worse; Hades, after all, is a god of an entire domain himself, and close brother to the king of all gods.

The reasoning and perceived apathy of the sun's charioteer did little to raise Demeter's spirits. She cursed the sun, the underworld, and Zeus himself, imposing upon herself an exile and resigning herself to grieving. According to Homer, she took the form of an old woman in the city of Eleusis, which we know would become the site of her annual Mysteries. Taken in by the king of Eleusis' daughters, she became a confidant and midwife to the queen and was charged with raising the newborn boy Demophoon. According to the hymn, she fed the child neither milk nor solid food but anointed him with ambrosia, much in the same manner of Apollo. Unbeknownst to the mortal court, she would bathe the child nightly by fire to cleanse him and move him toward the path of immortality. Upon discovering this, the queen and her court snatched the young Demophoon from Demeter's care; this infuriated her. Dropping her disguise, she cursed the island with perpetual civil war. The harvest goddess then took her leave, vowing to build upon the highest hill a temple in her honor, where her rituals will be studied and performed each year to appease her wrath. Thus, the reason for the location of the Eleusinian Mysteries.

Alone in her Eleusinian temple, without daughter or newfound son, Demeter set once again to mourning. She plucked from the earth its fruits and grains, dried it to a husk, and left its cattle destitute. Her famine deprived the people of food and the deities atop Mount Olympus of their customary sacrifices. Her exploits upon the earth had, by this time, reached the ears and wounded the pride of Zeus, who had grown tired of Demeter's meddling in the mortal world. He dispatched Iris, a minor winged goddess, down to the Eleusinian temple to demand on Zeus' behalf Demeter's return to Olympus. Of course, Demeter denied the pleas of a perceived lesser deity. However, this did not dissuade the Olympians, who, annoyed that the population of the earth was no longer sacrificing in their honor, went one by one to Demeter's temple to demand her return. To each visitor, Demeter provided the same answer: she would neither return the bounty of the earth nor Olympus until her daughter had been returned to her.

Man was left without food to eat or sacrifice. As king of Olympus, it was Zeus' duty to find a suitable compromise between Hades and Demeter. To satisfy all parties, he proposed that while Persephone should remain Hades' wife, he could not possess her in the underworld alone, and she would be allowed to split her time between Hades' realm and alongside her mother. For one-third of the year, while Persephone was enclosed in the underworld, Demeter bestowed starvation and drought upon the earth, yielding the season of winter. When that season passed, Persephone brought with her in a sudden surge all the growth that had been repressed, aided in celebration by her mother. This we know as the season of spring, where the bounty of the earth once again comes to life.

Dionysus

In keeping with the theme of celebration, we are met by the lord revelry himself: Dionysus, the patron deity of festivals, wine, general carousing, and the theatre. Naturally, from these, we can infer that he also holds some sway over the "ritual madness" of intoxication; he is essentially the king of the drunks. He is often depicted completely nude, and unlike his Olympian brothers, not necessarily in the most chiseled shape. His form borders on the feminine; he is portrayed usually with soft features and hair that tumbles down his back and shoulders, though typically not unkempt. It could be argued that Dionysus is truly the most benevolent of all Olympians; certainly, he is the most difficult to anger.

Dionysus seems, compared to his Olympian counterparts, a proverbial "black sheep." He cares nothing for the struggles of man, is not so vain that he covets a mortal or divine position, and seems content to spend his days in repose with a glass of wine or twelve. The Ancient Greeks explain this stark deviation from the Olympian norm by asserting that Dionysus is, in fact, a foreigner, a Thracian by divine birth who essentially weaseled and charmed his way into the immortal halls of Mount Olympus.

As the god of celebration, Dionysus boasts an enormous domain; it touches nearly all facets of Greek society. He is present at weddings, funerals, harvests, and sacrifices, not to mention all religious rites and rituals. When oracles fall into their soothsaying trances, Dionysus, it is said, is pulling the strings.

As vintner of the gods and giver of fruit to mankind, Dionysus' symbols include the grape and its vines, the goat, the chalice, and a staff of fennel wound tight with ivy known as a Thrysis. Just like Demeter, Dionysus had an immense, ancient cult following across Greece that existed even before Homer. There is some speculation that, due to their similar realms, the Eleusinian Mysteries were devoted both to Demeter and Dionysus; this is supported by evidence of a large Dionysian following on the island of Eleusis.

Dionysus also claimed in addition to the Mysteries, the festivals of Dionysia and Anthesteria. The former was divided into two parts: the rural Dionysia, and the city, or "greater" Dionysia. Both shared the same purpose:

to celebrate the grape harvest throughout Attica, in gratitude for the gift of fruit Dionysus bestowed upon the Greeks. Plays and poetry recitations were held in honor of the god of revelry to celebrate, and naturally, the wine flowed freely. The Anthesteria, on the other hand, was a three-day festival that mirrored some concepts of modern-day Halloween. Though it was celebrated at the vernal as opposed to the autumnal equinox, it marked the days when the wine from the previous year was fit to drink, and thus induce the "ritual madness" which the Greeks believed thinned the barrier between the living and the dead.

Myths

Unlike his stationary Olympian siblings and counterparts, Dionysus was renowned as a chronic, compulsive wanderer, carrying with him the grapevine and the knowledge of how to cultivate it. It is said that Hera, Dionysus' mother, threw him into a fit of madness, which sparked his wanderlust; the myth states that throughout his travels, he left behind him swaths of vegetation and the knowledge of how to cultivate the grape. Some versions of the myth state that Dionysus' obsession with the grape stemmed from a love affair he had with a young man named Ampelos, who died falling from an elm tree following Dionysus' request that he guard the god's sacred vines. In his mourning, Dionysus turned his lover into the fruit that the vines produced and sowed it throughout the world in his sadness.

In his interactions with humanity, Dionysus tends toward the ambivalent, even the flippant, as opposed to his brothers and sisters, whose main motivation remains vengeance of selfishness. One of the most famous stories in the Western canon involves Dionysus, who causes a mighty king great sorrow and regret for choosing his words carelessly. The king Dionysus plays this cruel trick on is King Midas, whom Dionysus stumbles across while sowing his grapes and pressing his wine. Dionysus, impressed with Midas' generous hospitality, reveals himself as an Olympian god and allows the king one wish, to which we know exactly how the king replied. Unable to eat, drink, or hold his children, Midas despaired at his golden touch and begged the god of revelry to recant his wish. Dionysus agrees in good spirits and takes Midas down to a river, where he washes himself clean and turns the river golden.

Dionysus, being no stranger to madness, once descended blindly into the underworld to bring back his wife and mother from the realm of the dead. He did not know the way to the underworld, and in his travels, asked an old man named Hypolipnus for help. The old man, lovestruck by the handsome Dionysus, promised to show him the entrance to the underworld if the god, in return, promised to remain with his guide forever. Eager to rescue his family, the young Dionysus consented to the old man's demands. When he returned from the underworld, however, Dionysus discovered that the old man had died. On his return with his wife and mother to Mount Olympus, it is said that Dionysus picked up Hephaestus along the way, helping the deformed craftsman back into the immortal Olympian fold. The myth has been interpreted as a triumph of revelry and celebration of mortal life over the grimness of death, an ancient rendition of the old phrase, "Love conquers all."

Hestia

Arguably the most important peripheral deity in all Greek religion is Hestia, goddess of the home, the hearth, the family, and the state. Greek legend states that upon the christening of any new building or completion of any new house, the first sacrifice to be offered was to Hestia, to ensure the prosperity, security, and longevity of the structure and its inhabitants. Given the condition of the many remains of Greek buildings throughout the centuries, it could be argued that Hestia has done a fair job holding up her end of the divine bargain.

The ubiquitous Hestia has but one true symbol: the hearth and the fire within it. Hers is a simple, safe world devoid of ravenous animals or the terrors of the sky and water. Her goal is to provide comfort and community beneath a roof and behind a door. Her domain was the culmination of all the previous divine realms; the harvest of the grain from the earth having been completed, Hestia remained responsible for turning that grain into bread through fire and ensuring there was enough to feed and warm the household. She is the most closely human of the Greek Olympians in that humanity exercises just as much control over her realm as she does. Hestia provides wealth and warmth to a home equal to the amount of work a man puts into it.

Curiously enough, as prominent as Hestia was in Ancient Greek mythology, she never possessed standalone worship sites. Other deities had their temples and monuments, we know, but Hestia's temples were considered by the Greeks to be the fireplaces of every home and public building. That she had so diffused herself into Greek culture and custom gave rise to a mode of Greek thinking that placed her outside the twelve Olympians; in fact, it was said that she forfeited her place among her brothers and sisters to Dionysus to maintain cosmic harmony.

Hestia is the oldest and youngest of all the Olympians, according to the myth of Cronus' disgorging. She was the first daughter of Cronus and Rhea. Due to her seniority among the Olympians, she is often pictured in a subdued, mature fashion, a striking deviation from many of her Olympian counterparts. Above all the Olympian goddesses, she radiates a matronly air in many of her representations; she often appears cloaked and robed, complete with a head covering, and extending an arm with a beckoning finger. When the Olympians erected their temple atop that eponymous mountain and divided the world, Zeus instructed that Hestia would be charged with keeping the fires of the hall lit and hot with the discarded portions of animal sacrifices.

Myths

Though Hestia had arguably the greatest, most immediate presence of all her Olympian counterparts, there are surprisingly few stories involving her. We see that one reason for this is that she may not have been considered an official "Olympian," or perhaps that her duties as goddess of the hearth are essentially invisible. She works to make the home, family, feast, and warmth all plentiful, and as such, it seems she has no use for intervention on the lives of men. However, we do know at least one small myth addressing how she got her position as keeper of the divine hearth.

Like her sister Artemis, Hestia wished to remain chaste for eternity. It is said that at one point, both Poseidon and Apollo once sought to make a wife of Hestia. When Zeus was ready to commit his sister to the bonds of marriage, Hestia pled to let her stay on Olympus, which she loved above all, keeping the hearth of the massive temple warm and inviting. Swayed by her devotion, Zeus allowed her to stay, giving her the position not only of the divine homemaker but bestowed upon her the gift of every fireplace past, present, and future as an altar to her service. She would be placed "in the midst of the house and receive the richest portion [of all offerings]," according to Homer's hymn.

To Conclude

We see that our remaining Olympians hold a humble yet elevated presence compared to the other deities covered thus far. Each of our four holds control of a world that exists primarily in the material, and within those material worlds, the divine rulers work to ensure a better quality of life for mankind. These four are, above all, the most benevolent and charitable to humanity, bestowing upon them the technology, tools, and wisdom that allow for advancement through the ages and mastery of the harsh, oftentimes lethal natural world.

We see that all four of these divines are connected to the earth in more intimate ways than their counterparts. As mankind sprang from the clay of the earth, it is a small wonder that those gods whose tools and spaces are similarly tied to the planet would occupy a greater prestige in daily Greek life. These four deities provide the basis for interpersonal communication and celebration, linking the chains of ancient islands together with food and festivity.

Chapter 7:

The Love Below

It would appear at this point that we have hit a bit of a snag in rounding out our mighty Olympians; we are left with a proverbial "elephant in the room," or perhaps more fittingly, the "elephant below the room." We have omitted from our discussion thus far Hades and his domain, the underworld. There are multiple reasons for this. The most in line with Ancient Greek mythological and religious thinking is that Hades is technically not an Olympian; in claiming the underworld, he abdicated his seat among the gods in favor of full sovereignty and autonomy over the realm of the dead. The second reason, in keeping with the first, is that Hades' realm is so vast, touching so many facets of divine and mortal life throughout Greek mythology, that devoting an entirely separate chapter to its places, people, and stories seems almost necessary to begin to understand it.

Death, as in all ages, held especially peculiar importance to the Greeks. Given the terrors of the surrounding environment, the expansion of hostile forces through conquest, and that medical technology was next to nonexistent, the ancient Mediterranean people would have been surrounded by death for reasons beyond their comprehension. Naturally, based on their religious thinking, it would stand to reason that the Ancient Greeks would create an entire mythological ecosystem to attempt to answer the questions that seem to be incongruous with the behavior of their more visible and benevolent Olympian divines. To the Ancient Greeks, as to many other cultures, death was a sort of theft; a life was removed from the visible world. The questions then arose: Who stole that life? Where did they take it? It could not be the many Olympians who snuffed it from the mortal plane; while it is true that they were vengeful and oftentimes cruel, the Olympians were much more satisfied transforming humans than outright killing them. Nor could the life be taken by Mount Olympus, for only those deities could set foot there.

If lives undeniably disappeared but retreated neither to the top of Mount Olympus nor to Poseidon's depths, then, mythologically, the one remaining place they could go was the most mysterious and opaque of all: beneath the earth itself. It was a world unimaginable to the Ancient mind; from beneath the earth grew all life grew and withered, so logically there must be something there. What was that something; what did it look like? Who controlled it, and above all, did it mean to instigate violence against the living? The answers came in another, albeit shadowy, form of the divine: Hades, his black horses and strange abominable creatures, the god with least concern for mortal activity beyond claiming their souls to populate his gloomy underground kingdom which today shares his name.

Hades

Up until this point, we have mentioned the lord of the underworld as a passing character in several preceding myths; mostly, he has been a selfish, cunning character bent on abduction or theft to benefit himself. We have seen that it is essentially his fault we have winter, among other earthly misfortunes. Hades, sometimes referred to as the "Zeus of the Underworld," occupied a position certainly self-serving but surprisingly apathetic. The commonly held belief was that for all the evil Hades could inflict upon the earth, his primary desire was to maintain balance on the planet by offsetting his brother's actions.

Unsurprisingly, Hades had few sites of worship in Ancient Greece. Superstitious as they were, they avoided calling attention to the lord of the underworld as they were afraid of summoning him; taking an oath in his name may result in an untimely end for those who swore it. Bizarrely, however, all across Greece, he was nearly as revered as he was feared and loathed. We are told that he often received sacrifices and that in worship, Greeks would avert their eyes from his image and bang their heads against the ground to ensure that Hades would hear them.

It seems Hades left his estate beneath the earth only a handful of times in his mythos. Once, we know he departed to ensnare the young Persephone, but other than that, Hades seemed to remain covetous of his sovereignty and what he deemed a perfect, natural, and legal order. We are treated to many colorful descriptions of Hades' realm, particularly in Homer's works, where he describes the lord of the underworld's estate as "full of guests," which is, for all its macabre context, a pretty funny way to describe the eternal entrapment of souls. He was jealous of those who managed to escape his tyrannical legal system, who, coincidentally, always seem to be at least half-god. His love of order, justice, and balance is often his undoing; Hades is entirely his own master, but a slave to his own rules.

Myths

It seems that most of Hades' direct myths employ demigods; frankly, they seem to be stories where the half-divines outwit, outlast, or outrun the order-loving, law-abiding lord of the underworld. Heracles, Perseus, and Odysseus all took their turns confounding the rules laid out by Hades, who, with metaphorical hands tied and literal fists shaking, had no choice but to let them return to the upper world of the living.

One instance where Hades emerges a victor by his own design is in his dealings with Theseus, the mythical king of Athens. Having unrivaled power among the Greeks, Theseus, in his hubris, plotted with his best friend Pirithous, a Thessalian king, to take daughters of the gods for wives, as they could seemingly find no mortal woman that pleased them. Theseus kidnapped Helen of Troy, holding her hostage until she was of marrying age. Pirithous, foolish as he was, chose to kidnap Persephone. Having some degree of omniscience, Hades caught wind of the Thessalian king's plans and readied an immense feast. The two kings arrived and were met with hospitality to rival that found on Mount Olympus; though as they ate, Hades quietly unleashed serpents to bind the two to their chairs, where for eternity they would sit, their senses tempted by food, but their stomachs always empty.

Hades also plays an essential part in another extremely popular, surviving myth: the story of Sisyphus in his attempt to cheat death. The story goes that Sisyphus, the man with a self-proclaimed greater wit than Zeus, broke a promise to Zeus that he would not reveal the location of Aegina, an invisible nymph kept hidden by the king of the gods. Furious, Zeus ordered Hades to take Sisyphus down to his kingdom and chain him up as punishment. Having been escorted to the underworld, Sisyphus encounters Hades setting up the chains of punishment. Sisyphus asks Hades if he can show him how the chains work as a means of punishment, to which Hades obliges. Sisyphus then locks Hades up and flees back to the upper world, seemingly having bested death itself.

The problem arises when Hades is unable to fulfill his duties as the claimer of souls; if he is detained, nothing can die. The Olympians cannot receive their animal sacrifices, grain cannot be harvested, the old cannot pass on, and plague spreads, unhindered by the culling of its hosts. The earth is thrown into chaos, and Zeus takes notice. He sends a fuming Ares, no stranger to entrapment himself and furious that war has lost its fun, to free Hades from his chains, and deals with Sisyphus himself. The now famous punishment handed down to the king who cheated death was the eternal rolling of a boulder up a mountain, only to have it tumble back down to its foot.

Places of the Underworld

The underworld offers us an opportunity to glimpse the imagination of the Ancient Greek writers, unlike its exalted counterpart Olympus, of which we have scant physical descriptions. One reason for this may have been that many Greeks understood and agreed to some capacity what Olympus looked like, so rendering it upon a page or in a spoken poem would seem redundant or unnecessary. The underworld, however, was and still is a place of great mystery. Nobody has ever seen it, but given the many terrors that bring about death, one can imagine that the destination for those taken souls is anything but paradisiac. Comprising rivers dividing souls by their quality and fields wherein those souls spend eternity, the underworld's geography is rigid, severe, and abysmal.

The River Styx

The River Styx is the single most famous and recognizable locale in all the Greek underworld; behind Mount Olympus, it might be the most recognized in all Greek mythology. It is the river that supposedly separates the world of the living from the realm of the dead. It is an indispensable part of the underworld's ecosystem, as it provides the main highway of transportation into Tartarus for the newly deceased. As with many elements of the Greek mythological world, Styx is also personified as a nymph; she is a daughter of Oceanus punished by Zeus for siding with the Titans during the Titanomachy.

The Styx is one of five hellish rivers that converge upon the marshy center of the underworld; this is referred to as "the Styx," a term that today we colloquially carry to mean any backwoods, sparsely habited wilderness. We are told that the nymph and her fluvial incarnation can grant invulnerability to anyone who bathes there. In fact, it is said that as a boy, Achilles was dipped therein yet braced by his heel, later the location of his undoing by Paris' well-placed arrow during the Trojan War.

Tartarus

The deepest depths of Hades' realm, Tartarus can be described closest as a dungeon. To reach it, Hesiod says, would take nine days of descent from the plane of Hades, which in turn is nine days descent from the earth, which is nine days descent from Olympus. It is the paragon of the abyss; completely devoid of light and hope, it is the most severe punishment an eternal soul can undertake. Tartarus, in effect, is the "nothingness" of death. It is a vacuum from which there is no escape save divine intervention.

Naturally, Tartarus was deified, as is the Ancient Greek habit. He is one of the three original offspring of the cosmos; he is the middle child, stuck between his older brother Chaos and his younger sister Gaia. He is the one Greek deity whose realm remained intact after the Titanomachy; in fact, it is said that he guards the defeated Titans within his cells.

Those who inhabit Tartarus are said to be the most wretched of all beings; our cunning King Sisyphus is among them, eternally rolling his boulder. The Titans, as mentioned, take residence there, as does the king Tantalus, who, according to myth, murdered his son Pelops and served him as a meal when invited to dine with the gods upon Olympus. We can see that these are wholly unsavory characters, and Given Hades' love of justice, understand why they were fated to the chains of Tartarus.

Elysium & the Asphodel Fields

Though the punishments handed down may have been harsh and severe in many cases, for the most part, the underworld was less to be feared by the ordinary mortal. The worst of the worst were sent to Tartarus, but those who lived without severely offending the divines were sent to the Asphodel Fields.

The fields were described as flowery and peaceful, though not as we mortals would imagine. They were alive with blooms, certainly, but according to Homer, in his Odyssey, they were a dark place without joy or laughter. The impression one gets from the fields is that although one's mortal work may have ended, paradise in the afterlife remains reserved only for the divines.

On the other hand, those souls touched or deemed worthy by the gods would be escorted to Elysium, an exclusive paradise, which technically was separate from Hades' realm, but existed on the same plane. Elysium, split from its dismal underworld counterpart by the river Lethe, was a place of easy, bright, colorful life; stories state that there was always a light western breeze which kept the temperature manageable. Homer writes of Elysium that, in addition to the warmth, there is no snow, nor rain, nor drought; it is the perfect, ideal afterlife, though it seems populated almost entirely by demigods.

The River Lethe

Another one of the five rivers of the underworld, we know the mythical Lethe bordered Hades' domain and that of Elysium. It was the "river of forgetfulness," in that should one fall in or drink from it, their soul would forget everything it had known. It was a commonly held belief among those Ancient Greek cults of mystery that all souls drank copiously from the river before reincarnation. The story goes that as part of his punishment for trying to steal away Persephone, the king Pirithous was dropped into the river, thus wiping his memory completely.

The river traced its path around the interior of the underworld, looping the cave Hypnos, where wayward souls were drawn to sleep for eternity. According to some religious sources, the river has an opposite sister on the mortal plane named Mnemosyne, which provided those who drink from its waters omniscience and infallible memory.

The Rivers Cocytus & Phlegethon

Two of the remaining rivers both ringed the border of Hades, though they flowed in opposite directions: the Cocytus, the "river of wailing" or "river of lamentation," and the Phlegethon, the "river of fire." Both served to deter mortal interference and trespassing into Hades' realm, and both struck utter despair in the Ancient Greek imagination.

The Cocytus is unique among the underworld's rivers in that it varies in depth; this is because its purpose is to contain those souls who behaved traitorously or treasonously in their mortal bodies. Depending on how great the transgression, the backstabber could be submerged anywhere from their knees to above their heads; no matter how much water the victim takes on, however, they would be resigned to screaming and wailing for all eternity.

The Phlegethon is a more subtle river, despite its contents. It is a river of fire from which we draw some connotations of the Judeo-Christian ideas of "Hell" and its inferno. After winding around the border of Hades, the river plummets in a fiery cascade into the depths of Tartarus, the only of the five rivers to make that plunge. One myth surrounding the river of fire comes in relation to the nymph Styx. Supposedly, before being turned into rivers by the vengeful Zeus, Phlegethon and Styx were lovers before the Titanomachy. Having chosen the losing side in that conflict, the two were punished simultaneously. In turning into the river that bears her name, her physical being was consumed by the fires of Phlegethon, whom the retributive Hades charged with bordering his underworld. Not without his sense of justice, however, Hades, upon seeing the punishments carried out to a suitable conclusion, allowed the two rivers to be reunited in their meanderings through the underworld.

Two Flowers and a Dog

The locations of Hades' world provide a wondrously rich locale for the afterlife, and just as its cousins on the material plane, the rivers and fields are populated with all manner of symbolic plant and animal life. Some species of earthly vegetation, according to Greek myth, even originated in the underworld, and through either fruition or folly, wind up growing upon the earth.

Mint

One of the most intriguing stories of underworld flora comes in the form of the mint plant. According to the Greek myth, it is not a wholly earthly plant. Mint finds its roots in the underworld because of the all-too-common jealousy that pervades the ancient deities. The story goes that Hades, after marrying Persephone, falls in love with one of his subjects, a nymph of the river Cocytus named Minthe. Some accounts say that the nymph attempted to seduce Hades, who consequently fell under her spell. No matter how the lord of the underworld came to fawn over Mithe, Persephone would have none of it. Taking matters into her own hands, she transformed the nymph into the mint plant, scattering it across the underworld and the mortal plane, giving it so strong an odor and taste that it repulsed all animals.

Jonquil

Growing along the banks of the famous Styx and throughout the Asphodel Fields are splatters of jonquils, also known as narcissus. The white petals and yolky centers sprouting in clusters throughout the underworld are named for the young man so transformed: Narcissus, the most vainly handsome of all Greek men. Having been turned into the flower for scorning those who loved him, he remained fragrant, striking, and poisonous, perfectly suited as a lure for the unsuspecting Persephone. As she was dragged away by Hades' chariot, Persephone, according to myth, clutched a handful of the flowers between her fists, and thus they took root all throughout the underworld.

Cerberus

One of the most fearsome and famous creatures throughout the Greek mythos, Cerberus was the fierce and loyal companion of Hades. He is pictured as a dog with multiple heads, ranging from three to one hundred, and most often sitting obediently at Hades' side when he is atop his throne. In some depictions, Cerberus is presented as a single-headed hound, albeit with hundreds of snake's heads slithering down his back. He varies in size, though it is commonly accepted that he is, at the very least, the size of a man and often much larger. Though he was Hades' best friend, he was tasked with the important job of preventing wayward souls from escaping Hades' underworld. He was like

Hell's guard dog, although he was supposed to keep people in instead of out.

The most well-known myth surrounding the hound of Hades involves the hero Heracles, who, as one of his twelve labors, is sent to the underworld to capture Cerberus. The hero arrives, confronts Hades by asking politely to forfeit his possession of the multi-headed hound. Ever the legislator, Hades agrees to part with Cerberus on one condition: that Heracles defeat the giant dog in combat without the use of his weapons. Heracles subdued the creature and dragged him to the surface of the material world, where it is said that the dog vomited, and from that, the poisonous monkshood plant sprouted its first flowers on the earth.

To Conclude

There are countless other locales, symbols, and varying stories within Hades' underworld; to dive any further into their depth and breadth would almost assuredly yield an entirely new book, which is not this book's objective. I have attempted to convey efficiently those outstanding stories and elements which form the foundation for discussion about the belief systems and symbols of the Ancient Greek afterlife; I hope that while this chapter has provided a coherent map of Hades' world, it leaves many landmarks undiscovered, so that the reader may embark on that journey themselves.

Chapter 8:

The "Half" and "Half-nots"

We have made great allusions to this idea of Ancient Greek religion gravitating toward a world more human than divine, but all that is essentially speculatory. Of course, it makes sense that early, sophisticated human beings would understand the control of the world in relatively simple terms: those universal human emotions and motivations. How could it be possible to bring the two worlds even closer together, to entirely bridge the mythological gap? The very idea of worship or religious ritual is insufficient; it only elevates deities above mankind. Oracularity, while mystical and mortal, provides less a bridge to the divine realm and more a connection to it, and indeed one that can be severed quite easily.

What if, then, for all their temptations to control the lives of men, the gods were responsible for the birth and rearing of mortal men? Where would they rank? Surely, they are not fully divine; and yet neither are they completely human. Is their purpose on earth to abet mankind, or dissuade it from more noble goals? Are they acting solely on behalf of their Olympian superiors, or might it be that given their humanity, they have a genuine altruistic side? Many questions emerge when considering those half-immortal humans, the demigods; we can find their answers sprinkled throughout their stories. They affirm not only the Ancient Greeks' belief in the strength of mankind but ours as well.

There are an exceptional number of demigods planted throughout Greek mythology. However, we must lend our focus to the most visible, whose stories have been told and rehashed throughout the ages; again, our job is to provide an introductory framework to the mythology. We will be focusing on Achilles, Heracles, and Perseus because they all share the common elements of divine birth, world-shaping tribulation, triumph over seemingly insurmountable odds, and most importantly, a multitude of surviving texts and contemporary allusions upon which to draw.

Achilles

Touted as the mightiest of all Greek warriors, the great Achilles played a pivotal role in the Trojan War, and as such, Homer's Iliad, the ancient poem centered on the legendary conflict. Son of the sea nymph Thetis and the king of the ancient nation of the Myrmidons, Peleus. There are several stories surrounding Achilles' conception, though one myth stands out due to its humor. It comes in Aeschylus' play Prometheus Bound, where Achilles' mother, the chaste Thetis, is said to have been pursued without rest by many of the Olympian divines. Hera, the wife of Zeus, one of the amorous gods, prophesied that the child Thetis bore would be infinitely stronger than his father and would usurp any claim his father had in the world. Upon hearing this, the Olympian gods immediately dropped their conquest ideas and forced Thetis to marry Peleus, a mortal king.

If we are not familiar with the stories of Achilles, we certainly are familiar with his fabled body part, the heel. It is said that Thetis, fearing the destruction of her only child at the hands of the Olympians, fled to Hades' underworld and the safety of her sister Styx, the river of invulnerability, and dunked Achilles beneath it, holding him by his heel and thus keeping it dry. As such, Achilles' heel remained the only vulnerable place on his entire body, and it is a term we carry today to mean a weakness in an otherwise seemingly strong entity.

As mentioned previously, Achilles was the central figure in the Trojan War, fighting on the side of the Greeks against Troy. We are told by Homer that Achilles arrived at Troy with fifty Myrmidon ships, each carrying fifty soldiers of his nation. After having engaged in several battles with the Trojans and their hero Hector, the Greeks under Achilles and his lifelong friend Patroclus had been pushed back to the beaches harboring their ships, whereupon Patroclus donned Achilles' armor and rallied his troops for a counterattack. It proved to be successful, forcing the

Trojans all the way back behind the famous walls of their city, though Patroclus was killed in the onslaught, and Achilles' armor was stolen by Hector.

Seeing his best friend downed in battle, Achilles is whipped into a rage. He demands of Hephaestus to craft him new armor, a new shield, and a new spear, and sets out onto the field of battle, where with his godlike invulnerability and proficiency in weapons slaughters every enemy soldier he encounters in search of Hector. Homer writes that his rage is so great that if the gods had not intervened, he would have single-handedly sacked Troy. Ultimately, Achilles finds Hector and chases him around the walled city several times before Hector sees his fate is inescapable. Accepting his death, he begs Achilles to let his body be treated with the respect of a fallen warrior; Achilles does no such thing, tying Hector's corpse to the back of his chariot and dragging it around the battlefield in front of Troy. With his last breath, however, Hector prophesies the downfall of the legendary Achilles: that later in the war, Hector's brother Paris' arrow would bring about the hero's destruction.

Analysis

In this brief story of Achilles, as with many of the stories of the Greek demigods, what we see is the strength of humanity when inspired through the divine. In Achilles' case, he is brought to a godlike rage and seeks his revenge, not through any direct offense to him, as would be the case with Zeus or Poseidon, to name two, but because one of his closest friends has been unjustly slain in battle. We see that the gods themselves must intervene against the strength of one man, who is driven not only to great deeds on the battlefield but great shame in his desecration of Hector's body. This shows that although there is nobody on earth more powerful than this single, half-human warrior, he is dominated by those dark shades of humanity which haunt all mortal men.

Heracles

If Achilles is the most legendary Greek warrior, the place of greatest hero must belong to Heracles. Arguably the most famous figure in Greek mythology, Heracles' stories are blooming with rich symbolism of mortal strength and determination. He is, by all accounts, the divine protector of mankind, acting as the bridge between the mortal world and Mount Olympus. It is upon his shoulders that the fate of humanity rests, and he is, above all, its greatest champion; we can imagine him simply as an Ancient Greek Superman. His labors and conquests have helped shape the Western literary canon. His myths have been told and retold throughout history, but always point to the belief that mankind possesses those unique qualities of tenacity and internal fortitude that put even the seemingly divine efforts well within mankind's reach.

The result of Heracles' birth was one of Zeus' many extramarital affairs. Among the many stories of Heracles' conception, we are told that Zeus seduced the mortal Alcmene by disguising himself as her husband. Hera, knowing full well the affair had taken place, and true to her character, plotted vengeance not against her husband, but against her half-human offspring. She sent into the crib of the young Heracles a pair of snakes to dispatch the hero, although to no avail. Heracles' divine strength and constitution, even as a baby, prompted no fear but an instinct of domination; he was found by his earthly mother playing with the snakes as though they were toys. Astounded by the sight, Alcmene summoned Tiresias, a soothsayer, who foretold that the child would fulfill the destiny of a god, that he would be the conqueror of countless creatures.

Heracles' story picks up again when, as a young man, he killed his music teacher Linus with a lyre, and thus was forced from the city into the role of a shepherd, where he was supposedly visited by the divines in the form of two travelers. One offered the young Heracles a life of ease and pleasantness, one without severe conflict or great reward; this was Vice. The other, Virtue, offered the hero a difficult, harsh existence, one plagued with strife and brutality, but for all his struggle, he would be thrust into the halls of glory, with a seat on Olympus as his ultimate prize. Naturally, we can gather, Heracles chose the latter and propelled himself along the track that would yield his legend.

We are told that after choosing the path of Virtue, Heracles married the king Creon's daughter Megara, and had ten children. Driven to a fit of madness by the divine saboteur Hera, he winds up killing his family, his wife included. Heracles then wandered the earth, ultimately curing his madness at the Oracle of Delphi, of whom Hera had taken control. She instructed Heracles that, to atone for his crimes, he should lend himself to the service of the king Eurystheus for ten years, one for each slain child, and fulfill any request or task the king demanded of him. Other stories state that the service was a result of a compromise between Zeus and his vengeful wife; that if Heracles should complete twelve nigh-impossible tasks, he shall have proven worthy of immortality. Either way, we are given the meat of Heracles' life: his Twelve Labors.

There are many sources readily available regarding Heracles' Twelve Labors. Thus, it would be tedious to focus on them individually; as such, we will cover them briefly, though the reader is encouraged to seek out these stories on their own. According to myth, the tasks Eurystheus bestowed upon Heracles were accomplished with Athena's help, who had taken an interest in the hero's life. He was to, in varying order, slay, capture, and steal his way to freedom. He would be pitted against the terrible Hydra, the aggressive and vigilant Amazons, and the ever-defecating three thousand cattle of Augeas. He relies on his divine strength and human intelligence to bind horses' mouths shut, scare off man-eating birds, lie in wait to capture seemingly elusive beasts, and swipe golden apples from a jealously guarded orchard. His final impossible task, we know, was conjured up by a fearful Eurystheus who had grown wary that Heracles would, in fact, complete all his labors. He was to descend into the depths of the underworld and bring back Hades' multi-headed guard dog Cerberus, which he does, successfully evading death and earning his prophesied place atop Olympus.

Analysis

While there are many more stories surrounding Heracles, the ones mentioned occupy a space in the imagination that is as permanent as his seat of immortality. The common thread that strings these myths together is Heracles' human traits. Even after being driven mad by Hera, he accepts his guilt, takes responsibility, and seeks to make amends for his transgressions. He learns to be patient, clever, and diplomatic; he comes to rely less on his divine, unmatched physical strength, and more on his mortal traits. Therefore, due to his commitment to self-improvement, Athena takes an interest in his development. What we can learn from Heracles' stories is that it behooves a person to become well-rounded and fully developed. It is not simply enough to be gifted with great talent; it is necessary to cultivate those strengths and mitigate those weaknesses which a person is given in life, because, even if someone is born half-god, nobody is perfect.

Perseus

The oldest of our demigods, mythologically speaking, is Perseus. Before the days of the famous Heracles, Perseus was widely regarded as the greatest monster slayer in history. A contemporary of Bellerophon, Perseus is the only demigod who, in his mortal life, occupied a place of royalty; he was the king of the ancient nation of Mycenae and the Perseid dynasty, of which an unborn Heracles was prophesied to inherit. Though he was of divine birth, it seems that Perseus relies less on the help of his Olympian family and more on his own native intelligence and strength; he is truly the picture of a good king, eager to raise arms only in defense of the weak and in the name of justice.

The story goes that Perseus was a son of Zeus and Danae, daughter of the king of Argos. As is common, it was prophesied that the king would be overthrown by the impossible strength of his son, and as such, he imprisoned both Perseus and his mother in a wooden casket and floated them out to sea. Thanks to a prayer from Danae, the two washed up unharmed on the shore of Seriphos, where they were taken in by the king Polydectes.

As Perseus grew, he noticed Polydectes shower his attention and affection upon his mother, which he felt was ignoble, as he deemed the king a less than virtuous man. Polydectes, true to Perseus' assumptions, planned to thwart the hero's defense of his mother by fabricating grounds to dispatch him. He held a sprawling feast, asking that all guests bring a gift; specifically, the king demanded that all guests bring a horse. Having no horse to offer, the noble Perseus promised to bring the king any other gift he could possibly want; Polydectes, deeming it impossible, requested of Perseus the head of the Gorgon.

Perseus set to planning his impossible task; no mortal had approached the Gorgon and lived, much less taken its head. In his dismay, he was visited by the goddess of wisdom and strategy, Athena; she had taken a special interest in Perseus as a dedicated man of his word and offered the hero her divine assistance. Athena knew, as she was the one who turned Medusa into a Gorgon, exactly how to defeat it. She guided Perseus to the Greae, the three much older "grey sisters" of Medusa, who, sitting in a circle atop a mountain, shared one eye for seeing and one tooth for speaking. The Greae, according to myth, knew not only the whereabouts of Medusa but the tools to destroy her as well. Though the three refused to willingly give up their sister, Perseus, with his natural smarts, took from the three their only eye as they were passing it between them, holding it for collateral and promising to return it once his quest had been completed.

Perseus ultimately found the secret orchard of which the Greae spoke and collected a knapsack which could contain the Gorgon's gaze. He was given Hermes' sandals and sword and Hades' helm of invisibility; Athena furnished him a divine shield. With Athena's aid, he found the Gorgon's cave, and with his divine tools, severed its head; according to some stories, Pegasus winged horse flew from the Gorgon's neck.

Analysis

What we see in Perseus' encounters is the humility of the human spirit. True, he is gifted as his descendent Heracles with unrivaled strength and mettle, but Perseus differs in that his great labors are essentially selfless and for the benefit of others. He is an excellent judge of character, and although he does not see eye-to-eye with Polydectes on moral issues, he understands his place in the king's court and is grateful for the life the king has provided for him.

Perseus also embodies the noble human traits of honesty and accountability. He vows to return to the king the head of the Gorgon, and does just that, despite the ulterior motives of Polydectes. Sure, he steals the eye of the Greae, but only to vow to return it when his quest is complete, which he does. He is the picture of the upright and admirable human being; he does not seek glory to immortalize his own name, but rather to elevate those around him. These are the very traits that give him the sympathetic benefit of the gods; he is, in a way, the Greek mythical embodiment of "karma," getting from the world exactly what he puts in.

To Conclude

We can see that the demigods of Ancient Greece, and these three, in particular, possess those traits which even today we deem as most noble; they are generous, ambitious, hounded by determination, and tenacious in their pursuit of success. However, in their fallible humanity, they also claim those shadowy pieces of personality that dwell deep within us all: they are, in some instances, naïve, rash, and irrational; full of pride and short-sighted, they tend to rush headlong into conflict, and only afterward evaluate their judgments. They are characters whose explicit purpose is to amplify both the human and the divine; they are completely hyperbolic, and yet their presence sparks within us some sympathy, for their reasons in their struggles are not unfamiliar to us, though the situations and creatures might be.

Chapter 9:

"It Came from the Greek!"

We have seen that there is a plethora of intriguing myths regarding the creation of the earth, those divines who watch over it, and those chosen heroic individuals who act on behalf of and to benefit mankind. In addition to those wonderful personifications, the Ancient Greeks gave us a bestiary of unparalleled imagination. For all the huffing and puffing and pushing and pulling that the Olympians cause upon the earth, it is the creatures of Greek mythology that truly inspire the awe or fear of the worshipper.

The creatures of Greek mythology are some of the most iconic and inspired in any system of beliefs. What strikes the reader about these creatures is that while they apparently occupy a world of the imagined, there is always some relative plausibility to their existence. One can place them in the uncanny valley of believability; we know nowadays that they do not exist, but to the Ancient Greek mind, with all the tumult and unknowns the material world hid from the eye, who could say whether or not a creature with several different animal heads could exist?

In this chapter, we will be taking a closer look at several of the most prevalent beasts in Greek mythology: the centaur and its variants, Pegasus, Chimera, and the Hydra. All of these creatures hold a concrete place in the Greek mythos; each were so much a part of Greek religious thinking that they had developed their own narratives alongside their divine and semi-human counterparts.

Centaur & Demihumans

The centaur, it could be argued, is the most sophisticated of all Greek creatures; indeed, it is the closest to mankind, and even provides guidance and wisdom to the two-legged race, according to some stories. The centaur is a cross between a horse and a man; its lower body is equine, while from the waist up, it is decidedly human, thus endowing it with the powers of speech and reason. While they do possess the noble human traits of communication, many Grecian myths portray them as primarily brutish and animalistic; in some sense, they can be interpreted as the opposite manifestation of the demigod. Some scholars have taken their split form to represent early humanity's split between their instinctual, purely animal past and the cerebral, more analytical present and future. Still, others more historically oriented claim that the centaur is a misfired memory: that the creatures were in a sense "real," but were simply nomadic horsemen misremembered.

Chiron

The most well-known of all centaurs is Chiron, the mentor of Achilles and guardian of Prometheus. Apollo's son, Chiron, was held in great esteem among his half equine brothers because he was deemed the wisest and most measured of them all. As his brothers lived according to their animal instincts, debasing themselves with carnal pleasures and intoxication, Chiron devoted his time to artistic and intellectual development. He was renowned for his mastery and skill in healing, medicine, and the hunting arts, so much so that he is attributed throughout the pantheon as the inventor of botany and herbal remedies.

Even his appearance differed from that of his brothers. Chiron possessed more human elements than the average centaur; in depictions of the mythical beasts, one can always tell which Chiron is by his human front legs. In effect, he was an entire human with half a horse attached to his back, while other centaurs claimed all four hooves. We can read that Chiron possesses these distinctly human features because he is, through his actions and behavior, more human than animal, though he acts as the connecting bridge between man and nature, as is evident through his teaching.

Minotaur

A creature that belongs to the same category as the centaur is the Minotaur, the great bullish beast of King

Minos. It has the inverted physical qualities of the centaur: its body remains fully human, while its head takes the form of a bull's. It also has the bull's tail. The Minotaur is said to be the reason why the great inventor Daedalus created the labyrinth, the halls of which the Minotaur supposedly wandered as its prison.

The story of the Minotaur begins when King Minos, in competition with his brothers for Poseidon's favor and control of the kingdom, set to sacrifice a bull in the name of the sea god. Upon retrieving the animal, however, Minos noted how beautiful it was and kept it for himself, sacrificing a lesser animal to Poseidon. Catching wind of this, Poseidon, furious as always, swore vengeance on the king and made Minos' wife Pasiphae fall in love with the beautiful animal. Pasiphae then recruited Daedalus to construct a hollow cow made of wood so that she could mate with the bull. Thus, the Minotaur was born. Under protest of his wife, who loved the child, Minos could not bring himself to kill the bullheaded child. He had Daedalus construct the legendary labyrinth, where the Minotaur stayed until Theseus descended it and killed the beast.

Satyr

The third half-animal varies from its counterparts in many ways. The satyr, unlike its centaur and minotaur cousins, is fully divine. It is a forest spirit, often pictured with the ears and tail of a horse, and short, stubby hoofed and hairy legs like that of a donkey. They are depicted as walking upright, often dancing or in possession of an instrument: typically, a lyre or a pan flute. In some instances, they are lent the traits of a goat such as horns, as well as the occasional hyperbolic erection.

More closely related, mythologically speaking, to the nymph than the centaur, the satyrs are the forest spirits of the Ancient Greek world; they are symbols of youth, joy, new growth, and harnessed animal passion. They are known as devout followers of Dionysus and are imagined throughout plays and myths as possessing an insatiable sexual appetite, a taste for wine, and above all, a desire to play tricks and pranks on mortal men and women. All these traits are distilled down to their essence in the manifestation of one iconic satyr alone: Pan.

Pan

Pan is the very picture of a satyr in that he is the god of the field, the cave, springtime, improvisatory music, and sexuality. He is a mentor and teacher, though not with his mischievous side. It is from his stories that we are given the myth of the pan flute, and in fact, his name lends itself to our word panic.

We are told, due to his satyr's appetite, that Pan once attempted to seduce the nymph Syrinx, a devout follower of Artemis, and thus devoted to chastity. The story goes that Pan chased the nymph through the forest, and Syrinx, unwilling to yield but unable to keep running, transformed into a reed nestled within a marsh. When Pan came across the marsh and reeds, a breeze blew through them that made a sound that enchanted Pan's ears. Not knowing which reed his desirous Syrinx had turned into, he plucked several of varying lengths, tied them together, and blew through the ends of all, creating the pan flute.

In addition to his musical inspiration, Pan also claims total victory on behalf of the Olympians during the Titanomachy. As the war was raging, Pan claims in one of his stories, he was taking a nap in a field beneath a tree, as he can often be found. The action of the combat, or perhaps a stray thunderbolt, apparently disturbed his sleep so suddenly that he woke with a start and let loose his divine voice. Pan shouted, so loud, he claims, that he startled the Titans; they fell off Mount Olympus all the way into Tartarus. As we can see, this is where panic arose into the common vocabulary.

Pegasus

A famous symbol in the world over, Pegasus the winged horse occupies a pivotal part in Greek myths; he is seen at the side of a multitude of ancient heroes, aiding them in their seemingly impossible tasks. He is regarded as a symbol of man's triumph over nature as well as a manifestation of purity of heart and motive. He is commonly believed to be completely white, with wings that are usually pictured as larger than the horse itself sprouting from its foremost shoulders. When his powerful hooves strike the ground to launch himself skyward, some myths say, springs rush forth from the earth.

It is said that Pegasus is either one of the many offspring of Poseidon, or, as we have illustrated earlier, born immaculately from the blood of the Gorgon's neck. One myth that reconciles the two stories is that Pegasus emerged from the Gorgon's blood as it trickled into the sea, so that, in a similar fashion to the birth of Aphrodite, the horse sprang forth without a true "father," though Poseidon had a hand in his creation.

Regardless of his birth and parentage, we know for certain that the winged horse's guardian was the goddess Athena; who better to stable mankind's greatest ally than the divine most inclined to lend humanity a hand? Whoever Pegasus is charged with assisting on any given day, we can be sure that the myths provide our hero with a path through Athena. Some stories state that after Pegasus sprang into being, he made a beeline straight for the birthplace of thunder and lightning, by the side of Zeus within the clouds. There, in Zeus' pastures, the goddess Athena is said to have tamed him under the king of the gods' instruction, and thus became the sole master of the winged horse.

Bellerophon, one of the great pre-Heraclean heroes, for example, was united with Pegasus when he was charged with the task of dispatching the Chimera. The story goes that, unable to ascend the mountain wherein the Chimera lived on his own, he was instructed by the soothsayer Polyeidos to spend the night in the Athena's temple, which he did. The goddess came to him in his dream and bestowed upon him a golden bridle, and when Bellerophon awoke, he found that it had materialized. He came across the elusive winged horse at a spring, and ultimately tamed him using Athena's gift. Pegasus helped Bellerophon destroy the Chimera with immense ease, although the manner of his victory gave the hero an inflated sense of self-worth, and he began to think himself equal to the gods. To thwart his hubris, Zeus struck Pegasus with a gadfly while Bellerophon was riding him, and the winged horse threw the hero from his back, where he crashed to the earth, breaking his body.

Pegasus played his part in Perseus' rescue of Andromeda as well; he is an integral part of that most famous of Greek myths, which has been told and retold on page and screen many times. Part of that story involves the hero tracking the winged horse to where Athena had tamed it, and, seeing Perseus in need of a steed and deeming his character worthy, offers up Pegasus to the hero.

In addition to his role as helper to heroes, Pegasus was a necessary sidekick to the king of the gods himself. We know from several stories that Pegasus' role was to carry Zeus' thunderbolts and other weapons into battle.

He also shared the same responsibilities as Zeus' fabled giant eagles as a divine peacekeeper and an agent of mortal surveillance.

Chimera

The Ancient Greeks seem to associate the sinister or ungodly with deformations, amalgam and unbalance. This is made evidently apparent in their imaginings of the Chimera, a terrifying three-headed beast that lived in a cave atop an enormous mountain. Some stories claim it is the explanation behind the volcano, others that its purpose was to guard some unearthly treasure. Whatever its reason for being, it is arguably one of the most horrible and vicious creatures conjured up by the Greek imagination.

One of the reasons the Chimera strikes such fear into the Ancient Greek mind is that it makes its home on the mortal plane; Cerberus, the sea serpent, and Hydra, while all equally sinister, cannot be encountered by mankind during their earthly travels. The beast boasts the fire-breathing head of a lion, from its flank the head of a goat, and its tail the head of a snake. It is a porridge of creatures who share one thing in common: for one reason or another, they are to be feared by man.

Chimera, unlike many of its mythological family, was widely accepted and depicted as a female creature. It is written that Chimera was mother to the Egyptian Sphinx and Nemean lion, that massive beast slain by

Heracles as his first labor. We are told that Chimera's homeland was Lycia, in modern day Turkey, where several geothermal features have been long referred to as "the eternal fires of Chimera."

Where most creature mythology depends on oral and written tradition, the stories of Chimera are interesting in that they are predominately told through artistic expression; while Homer and later sources make mention of physical descriptions of the Chimera, source materials regarding her stories survive primarily on vases, jewelry, and other shards of pottery. This could be because, as an essentially "foreign" creature, the conception of Chimera was brought into Greece, wherein it flourished and disseminated throughout Greek culture, though was never entirely codified into the mythology. The myths tend to support this, in that Chimera is a foreign, unknown, and seemingly insurmountable and yet wholly mortal foe, who is vanquished by the "homegrown" Bellerophon with the aid of the decidedly Greek pantheon.

Hydra

The giant many-headed reptile known as the Lernaean Hydra was the victim of Heracles' second labor, and for good reason. The snakelike monster was a terror to those of Ancient Greece, said to possess not only intelligence but, by some accounts, the ability to regenerate entire portions of its body.

The creature was said to be the most poisonous and lethal of all mythical beasts; even its scent, in some stories, was lethal. It had disease-carrying blood and toxic breath and was outfitted with hundreds of razor-sharp, venomous teeth. Though the number of its heads varied according to different sources, some placed them at three, others fifty, it is agreed that the creature was gargantuan in size and would regrow two heads for every head it lost.

Hydra's mythological home was the lake of Lerna, somewhere on the eastern portion of the Peloponnesian peninsula. The lake is significant as a location of myth as it was considered one of the many entrances to the underworld, and as such, is one of the gatekeepers to Hades' realm. According to myth, the many-headed Hydra is the only creature under Hades' domain who lives primarily outside of the underworld itself.

The Hydra met its end, as we know, when Heracles vanquished it as one of his Twelve Labors. As the creature's scent alone could have killed him, he covered his mouth and face with a sheepskin so he would not breathe the noxious gasses emitted by the creature. Then, having snuck up on Hydra, Heracles severed its heads and deemed the labor complete. Hydra, on the other hand, was not quite vanquished, growing twice as many heads as Heracles removed. Seeing his predicament, and quickly becoming overwhelmed, Heracles called upon his nephew Iolaus to help him. With his nephew's aid, Heracles brandished a sword of fire and cauterized each wound he inflicted upon the

Hydra's various necks, thus thwarting its potential growth. Having slain the creature, Heracles then dipped his arrows in the Hydra's bile, thus poisoning them. The resulting wounds would be unable to heal.

To Conclude

The bestiary of Ancient Greek mythology is brimming with truly inspired creatures. Even those neglected in this brief account hold a mystique that sparks the imagination and provokes eternal questions about the ancient Mediterranean. Logically, these creatures could not exist in a literal sense; what, then, were they? Were they misremembered human beings? Or, like the fabled caught fish that keeps growing larger, some encounter with a literal creature that became inflated to mythical proportions over time? Whatever the case may be, the bestiary at its most exquisite provides modern day human beings an intriguing and coveted glimpse into the more earthly fears and perceived perils of the average Ancient Greek.

Conclusion

Though the pantheism of Greece and its worshippers have all but vanished from the earth, we are fortunate to have been handed down through the centuries those cultural artifacts that tie us intimately to our past and connect us to the future. It is the imagination and longing to understand and interpret the world that the Ancient Greek pantheon bestowed upon us, the people of today.

In this nowhere near exhaustive work, we have begun a simple evaluation of those features most prominent in Greek mythology; hopefully, with some degree of success, those stories have been brought back to life, and their importance underscored. We have seen the creation of the world, the construction of humans, creatures, and the end of life itself condensed into a small space, but this by no means should betray or undervalue the complexities and nuances of the Greek pantheon or the Ancient Greek way of life. Indeed, any given element of the themes and stories discussed in this work are worthy of countless books and studies; in part, it is this very inexhaustible intricacy of Ancient Greek culture that has allowed it to survive through the ages despite shifting spiritual trends. With a crumbling marble hand outstretched, it reaches even now for speculation, holds tightly human history, and points toward art.

Through those tumultuous ages of human history, mankind has always seemed to turn its gaze backward to these classic, immortal subjects and stories. It seems that mankind looks back, less for the nostalgia of the polytheistic culture, but to help guide it forward through whatever seemingly insurmountable obstacle that faces it. From the stories of Ancient Greece, we draw hope, inspiration, and confidence that humanity is a noble species. In a sense, the myths of the Greek pantheon operate as the Athena to our Odysseus; we trust we have the knowledge and experience to see ourselves through hardship, but we certainly will not turn down a little outside help.

We have seen in our brief study several themes as omnipresent as the Olympians themselves: that youth is to be valued as much for its energy and beauty as age is for its wisdom and experience, that pride, of all folly, is most rewarded with pain, and that although the world may be a hostile, destitute, and inhospitable place, family and community can greatly ease that burden.

We have become acquainted with the physical symbols of the Ancient Greek divines: their trees, animals, weapons, and clothing, and how and where their images were codified throughout Greece so that even today, they are immediately recognizable. We can identify Hermes, Hades, and Hestia at first glance, and can even explain to a certain extent why they are pictured the way they are.

We have constructed a bridge between the worlds of the divines and their supplicants, showing that for all the fear and respect the Ancient Greeks placed upon their deities, they had the utmost faith in the power of mankind to craft his own destiny and bear his own moral responsibilities. We see that although the Olympian gods are by no means accountable for their wrath and destruction, the sources of these outrages are undoubtedly human emotion.

Although the Greek pantheon has a reputation for the fantastic, the otherworldly, and the truly impossible, when we take a closer look at it, we see that though the conclusions about the world and its mechanisms tend to be farfetched, the reasons and logic behind those conclusions is, by ancient standards, quite sound. Creatures were not simply brought out of the imagination from fear, but with the intent of a measured explanation of a phenomenon or event. Natural disasters and even precise locations are usually explained as the result of a god or goddess' particular action or as a consequence thereof, not because their omniscience "willed it" into being.

Beyond any religious fervor or ideology, truth or falsehood, the Ancient Greek mythologies have handed down through the centuries the timelessness of narrative and storytelling. While we no longer look to explain the world through the inner machinations of naked, angry, invisible overseers, we are somehow still drawn to those ancient themes, symbols, and names that resonate within our imaginations. We carry the forms and structures of these ancient narratives into our modern-day storytelling; even the myths themselves have been reshaped and retooled to fit our contemporary sensibilities. Where the sciences of today are accustomed to explaining the world in the strictest, most technically accurate terms, they still acknowledge the importance of the Greek mythos through its nomenclature.

It is through the Greek myths, their characters and places that allow us to see deeper into ourselves as a species, and thus understand the world in a more holistic way. In that sense, the mythology of the Ancient Greeks is alive and well; it still serves its primary purpose of elaborating and expanding the world around, beyond and behind us, albeit in a far less dogmatic fashion. We see that, despite the near constant fluctuation in views, customs, nations, and languages across time and space, there is one thing from which we are never very far removed: the belief that above all, it is the power of the human imagination which can shape the world.

References

Aeschylus, & Griffith, M. (1983). *Prometheus bound.* Cambridge, UK: Cambridge University Press.

Apollodorus, & Frazer, J. G. (2002). *Apollodorus: The library: With an English translation.* Cambridge, MA: Harvard University Press.

Apollodorus, & Frazer, J. G. (n.d.). Apollodorus, Library Sir James George Frazer, Ed. Retrieved August 20, 2020, from http://www.perseus.tufts.edu/hopper/text?doc =urn%3Acts%3AgreekLit%3Atlg0548.tlg001.p erseus-eng1%3A1.2.1

Apollodorus, Higino, C. J., Smith, R. S., & Trzaskoma, S. (2007). *Apollodorus' Library and Hyginus' Fabulae: Two handbooks of Greek mythology.* Indianapolis, IN: Hackett Publishing Company.

Bulfinch, T. (1913). *Bulfinch's Mythology: The Age of Fable the Age of Chivalry Legends of Charlemagne.* New York, NY 1913: Thomas A. Crowell Company. Retrieved from http://www.gutenberg.org/files/56644/56644-h/56644-h.htm

Burkert, W. (1985). *Greek religion: Archaic and classical.* Oxford, UK: Blackwell.

Callimachus, Mair, A. W., Mair, G. R., Lycophron, & Aratus. (1921). *Callimachus and Lycophron.* London, UK: Heinemann. Retrieved 2020, from https://archive.org/details/callimachuslycop00calluoft

Callimachus. (n.d.). CALLIMACHUS, HYMNS 1 - 3. Retrieved August 20, 2020, from https://www.theoi.com/Text/CallimachusHymns1.html

Clayton, P. A., & Price, M. (2015). *The seven wonders of the ancient world.* London, UK: Routledge.

Diodorus, & Thayer, B. (n.d.). (Book III, continued). Retrieved August 20, 2020, from http://penelope.uchicago.edu/Thayer/E/Roman/Texts/Diodorus_Siculus/3D*.html

Frazer, J. G. (1994). *Studies in Greek scenery, legend and history: Selected from his Commentary on*

Pausanias' "Description of Greece". London:
RoutledgeCurzon. Retrieved from
http://www.gutenberg.org/files/56002/56002-h/56002-h.htm

Grant, M., & Hyginus. (2019). Hyginus, Fabulae.
Retrieved August 20, 2020, from
https://topostext.org/work/206

Hadas, M. (1950). *A History of Greek Literature*. New
York, NY: Columbia University Press.

Herodotus, Flower, M. A., & Marincola, J. (2002).
Herodotus: Histories. Cambridge, UK:
Cambridge University Press.

Hesiod, & Lattimore, R. (1991). *Hesiod: The Works
and days, Theogony, the Shield of Herakles*.
Ann Arbor, MI: University of Michigan Press.

Homer, Fagles, R., & Knox, B. M. (2001). *The Iliad*.
New York, NY, NY: Penguin Books.

Hurwit, J. M. (2001). *The Athenian Acropolis: History,
mythology, and archaeology from the Neolithic
era to the present*. Cambridge, UK: Cambridge
University Press.

Morford, M. P., Lenardon, R. J., & Sham, M. (2011). *Classical mythology*. Oxford, UK: Oxford Univ.- Press.

Sealey, R. (2003). *A history of the Greek city states: Ca. 700-338 B.C.* Berkeley: Univ. of California Press. Retrieved from https://books.google.com/books?id=kAvbhZr v4gUC&hl=en

Simon, E. (1983). *Festivals of Attica: An archaeological commentary*. Madison, WI: University of Wisconsin Press.

Smith, W. (n.d.). A Dictionary of Greek and Roman Biography and Mythology. Retrieved August 20, 2020, from http://www.perseus.tufts.edu/hopper/text?doc =Perseus%3Atext%3A1999.04.0104%3Aalphab etic+letter

Made in the USA
Las Vegas, NV
26 November 2021

35289161R00199